Making More Money for YOU!

Mutual Fund Investing on a Budget for Beginners

By Magnus Carter

3

content within this book has been derived from various sources. Please consult a licensed professional before attempting any techniques outlined in this book.

By reading this document, the reader agrees that under no circumstances is the author responsible for any losses, direct or indirect, which are incurred as a result of the use of the information contained within this document, including, but not limited to, — errors, omissions, or inaccuracies.

Table of Contents

Chapter 7 – How Often Do I Check on My Money?
143

Introduction

It is a shame that many people miss out on amazing money-making opportunities simply because they are confused or too afraid to look outside the box. Are you one of those?

Do you want to learn about making more money with the money that you are already earning?

Are you burnt out by typing in cubicles and want to retire early?

Do investment strategies and books feel overly complicated and discourage you from investing?

Then, this book is for you. This book is going to show you how thousands of people have increased their wealth by following a common and effective method. By picking up this book, you have taken the first step in improving your life. Now, you just have to read and implement its teachings. Mutual funds are one of the most popular forms of investment, and they are exactly what you are looking for to grow your money.

Schools may have taught you a bunch of information but making and handling money is not one of them. When you graduate and are on your own, you make mistakes and learn how to manage money on the fly. Because of this situation, many young people are unaware of methods that generate passive income and only work jobs after jobs to earn financial security. If you talk to anyone successful, they will always encourage you to learn about investing because, despite the risks, it is a sure-fire way to gather wealth for the long run.

With advertisements and their popularity, you must have heard about mutual funds; however, if you have not, you don't need to worry because we have got you covered. In this book, the concept and working of mutual funds are described in very simple and easy steps. You will not find legal jargon flustered throughout the chapters. The book's purpose is to educate as many people as possible about the investing market and how to begin investing in your first dollars.

What type of mutual fund you will invest in will mostly depend upon your goals and how much you are willing to take risks. For example, buying bonds is riskier but has the highest returns. If your priorities are straight, then choosing a method will not be very difficult for you. You do not need to be an expert in the field yourself to get high returns through mutual funds, either. Whenever you purchase a mutual fund, the expenses also cover a professional that manages your fund's portfolio and helps you get the best out of your invested money. These plus other advantages have made mutual funds a favorite investing option for every class of assets.

Why should you believe me? My name is Magnus Carter, and I am an employee of a corporation. Just like you, I was raised with a mindset of working hard to earn money. When I was 17, I was already working at two fast-food joints and was slowly building up my wealth. I knew that I needed to build my financial record fast to live a stress-free and satisfying life. However, with this method, tiny progress was made. Then, I followed another popular piece of advice: going to college. After graduation, I had a bigger salary, but also my expenses. Again, I was making tiny progress. There is more to life than doing a 9 to 5 job so you can eat.

A successful friend of mine approached me one day and advised me to start investing. At first, I did not want to risk my hard-earned balance and rejected the offer, but he insisted. My first investment became a mutual fund, and I was perplexed by how easy it was. Within a year, I received profits that were hard to even think of. After retiring early, I made a mission in life to teach others about a life where you and your happiness matter more than your paycheck.

The first people I taught to invest were my close friends and family members. They always complained about money and gave colorful excuses for their shortcomings. This included a person living paycheck to paycheck, with the responsibility of a young child on her shoulders. After teaching her about building wealth, investing, and increasing her financial literacy, she has gained financial stability that will help not only her but also her child in the future. People come and thank me daily for help with their struggles, and I hope to do the same for you.

Mutual funds are a relatively low-risk investment option that people gain significant returns on. The biggest cause of stress is financial instability, and with this book and my advice, you will be able to live a better quality life, with less stress of money loaming around your head. You will be able to leave a better house and background for your children and grandchildren. Slowly but surely, you will see that working hard is not the only way to become independent. Investing is how rich people remain rich, and now you can apply them in your life also.

Do not sleep on this idea and leave this book unopened on your shelf. Many people get fooled and lose money on quick money-making schemes and suffer losses. This is not a quick money-making fraud scheme. You will be able to slowly grow a big balance through investing in a small fund or 'seed'. This will only grow with time and the best day to plant its seed is now. Many people get the idea of controlling their own lives but never put any actual study or practice into it. You will not get your first investment deal on a silver platter, and you need to work hard for one. Do not let the knowledge in this book go to waste, and start investing in mutual funds today.

How can I invest? This book is filled with chapters that step-by-step guide you to start a successful mutual fund portfolio for yourself. You will learn how to build your wealth so you can invest in mutual funds. The book will tell you about its different types, their risk-to-benefit ratio, and expenses related to it. I will inform you about all the fees and expenses you will encounter and help you identify fraud so you can quickly back away from it. All this and so much more is going to be revealed once you start reading. Every step is carefully stated, so do not delay and quickly uncover the knowledge in this book that can potentially change your life. And, I have enclosed the tools that will help with your journey. To get these tools send an email to mcarter@legendaryproductsandservices.com or you can download them here if you have the digital copy.

Chapter 1 – Finding My Buying Power

You might be feeling two emotions. You are either worried that you do not have enough money to invest and are afraid of losing money or are too excited to start participating in trade. Both of these mindsets are not very beneficial ways of thinking about your finances. In the former, you will never be able to change your net worth and will be stuck doing an office job at the age of 50. On the other hand, being too eager may put you at a higher risk of losing money, and you might end up hurting yourself.

What you need is to operate with a "balance" – a sort of goldilocks zone. Invest money that you are willing to risk and not use a big portion of your income, at least not immediately. You also do not want to invest such a small amount that your returns seem insignificant. This will keep a large portion of your finances secure and also allow you to work in the investing business.

How can you do that? It is quite simple. Unlike other books, whose intentions might be to glorify individuals and manipulate readers into buying a product, I will help you overcome your biggest concerns. Many experts do not teach others about their methods and techniques, but I will preach only what I practice. I started to invest using the tips mentioned in this chapter, and I hope, by following them, you will do the same. I will tell you how to set aside some capital for your investments. You will soon learn how to make a budget that gives you freedom of investing. To do this, first, you need to figure out your net worth and make an efficient budget.

Net Worth

Net worth is a number that measures your wealth. It helps you and others identify what kind of financial situation you are in. It is the value of your assets, everything you own, minus total liabilities. The bigger this number, the better your financial standing.

Asset

An asset is an item that has a financial value that belongs to you. This is your money in various forms. This includes your house, properties, equipment, patents, and cash in your bank. It also includes investments in retirement accounts, vehicles you own, and jewelry.

Liability

Liability is the sum of money you owe, either on your assets or debts. This includes mortgage, bank debt, tax owed, credit card balance, student loans, any other loan, etc.

In easier terms, net worth is a number that you are left with after you add everything of value that you own, including the value of your home to money saved in a bank account, and then subtract the money you owe in debts, like mortgage, student loans, and credit card. Another way to understand it is by imagining selling everything you owned and paying off all your debts. The cash you will be left with is your net worth.

Why Is Net Worth Necessary to Calculate?

When you are assessing your financial situation, you need to have a firm grasp of your net worth. You need to be aware of what liabilities you have and what you owe; otherwise, no matter how much money you make, you might go into debt. Secondly, it is a great way to track your progress. As you are investing, you will see how it positively affects your net worth and will give you peace of mind and stability. Thirdly, you can compare yourself to others, whether you are doing better or worse than the average person.

The Net Worth Of U.S. Families

The median net worth of a U.S. household is not adequate for them to retire comfortably. The net worth numbers spike at the age of 65; even then, house and property make up most of it. If you are younger, you will have a significantly lower or even negative net worth value because of lower salaries, student debt, and mortgages. This is not uncommon, and there is no need to panic.

If you calculate your net worth to be in the lower digits or negative, you might need to start finding ways to increase it. Having many investments and income supply is the key to growing wealth. There is no magic ubiquitous net worth number that you can strive for. It is important only to keep increasing it gradually and making yourself financially secure with each passing day.

How Can You Calculate Your Net Worth?

It is a very simple process; you just need to subtract one number from the other. However, the main thing is to gather all the information about the assets and liabilities you owned. You can do this on a piece of paper, but that can be lost or ruined. Instead, it is better to use a budgeting app or a dedicated spreadsheet that you will update yearly to get accurate information stored at your personnel at all times. Make a file or a folder for this exact purpose on your personal computer. This is what most financial experts themselves do and recommend.

Finding out and listing all this information can seem very hectic at first. Still, it is extremely important not only for you but also for your spouse and children. They might need it someday, and it will be beneficial that the file or folder is punctually updated.

A folder like this can change into a more in-depth assessment with the addition of records of money transfers, tracking of investment progress, and tax calculation. Calculating net worth, using the information of what you own and what you owe, can lead to you becoming more financially literate.

The **first step** is to calculate your assets.

1. List all the things you own in the order of most value. Make sure you are writing the amount according to recent and accurate estimates of the market and the dollar's value in the present. Start by writing down your largest assets. These can include:
    a. Value of your house
    b. Value of your real estate properties
    c. Car and other vehicles you own such as boats or bikes
    d. Cash value of any insurance
    e. If you own a business, they also add value to your business

2. Now, write down money saved into your accounts or other liquid assets. A liquid asset is something you own that can be quickly turned into cash for your use. These include:
    a. Money in checking and savings accounts (in case of multiple accounts), write them separately, e.g., the account of bank A, and then the account of bank B
    b. Value in investment accounts such as brokerage accounts and retirement accounts
    c. The money you have in cash form

3. Next, you have to list out personal belongings that may be of significant value. You do not need to list out every

piece of furniture, only those items that are worth more than $500. These include

    a.   Jewelry
    b.   Musical instruments
    c.   Coin collection
    d.   Heirlooms
    e.   Paintings
    f.   Gadgets or machinery
    g.   Rare wine collection

4. Lastly, you have to add all of the amounts mentioned in the above categories. The number you will get is the value of your total assets.

Tip: You have to be honest about the worth of your assets to get an accurate picture of your net worth. When writing values, be conservative and use lower estimates, especially with home and vehicle values.

The **second step** is to calculate your liabilities.

1. Like mentioned before, you will list things in the order of most owed to least. First, write down your biggest liabilities. Do not forget to write their current balance alongside them. These will include:

    a.   Insurance payments
    b.   Car loan
    c.   Mortgage

2. Now, write down the liabilities that you are currently adding as well. These will include:
    a. Student loans
    b. Credit card debt
    c. Any other personal debt

3. Again, add all the numbers mentioned in the categories. This number will represent your total liabilities.

Tip: By using an app or spreadsheet, the calculation can be done immediately.

Calculate The Net Worth

To get your number, simply minus the total liabilities amount from the total asset number. It does not matter how large or how small the number might be. If it is small or negative, now you have an idea about your financial situation. The first calculated net worth is just the starting point by which you can compare your future values.

The important thing is to keep calculating your net worth each year. By comparing this number with the net worth values you will calculate in upcoming years, you will get an idea of how you are progressing. You will know if you are lagging or increasing your wealth goals. To start a strict saving and debt repayment plan, you need to calculate this value more often, maybe every two months.

Now that you have calculated your net worth, you know how much work needs to be done. To increase assets, you can keep your savings in a high returning account, which will give more percentage of growth, especially if you are receiving a significant salary. To decrease liabilities, you can aggressively work on debt repayment and refinancing debts at a lower interest rate.

These little tips can help, but a major change can only come when you set an efficient budget and start investing.

Do you have enough money to invest? The chances are that you do but have no idea how you should be deducting your hard-earned cash. To recognize investment potential, you need to first set up an amazing budget.

Reaching your financial goals can look daunting in your mind, but with an efficiently calculated budget, you will not be so overwhelmed by it and become more motivated.

What is a Budget?

Your budget encompasses your monthly (or any period) household expenses and income. A budget shows the amount of money you are bringing in and compares it to the amount of money you are spending, e.g., rent, groceries, entertainment, etc.

When the word budget comes up, people assume it means to restrict spending and "no more spending on fun items," but that is not always the case. It should not be seen as a negative but a stepping stool towards a responsible financial life.

In dieting, eating broccoli for a week is less effective in keeping weight off than finding a delicious healthy dish you will eat for life. Budgeting is the same. Do not cap a restriction, but make a plan that is easy and realistic to follow.

How Does Budget Really Help?

With the help of a written budget for a month, you will plan how much you will spend and how much you will save that month. It helps you not to overspend and to make room for other expenditures.

Perhaps you do not want to limit your spending, and it can be scary for some people, but it has to be done. No matter how boring, it is key to keep your finances in order. If you limit your expenditures in one area, e.g., food, then you can build more wealth for a bigger purchase like a car. You could also save an emergency fund for rainy days and, most beneficial, save to invest.

Also, a budget can clearly show you where your money is traveling, e.g., where it comes from, how much it stays with you, and where it goes.

Making A Budget That Works

For starters, you need to get a firm grasp on your spending. You need to know what you can or cannot afford at present and what are your goals and priorities.

Visualize where you want to go and what you want to achieve. Is it to be debt-free, buy a house or build an emergency fund? A clear goal will help you determine what items are non-negotiable and which areas you can tweak. Create a financial roadmap in your head. Figure out roughly how much you can or need to live on. How much effort you need to give towards your financial goals, and for how long. Estimate a bare minimum you can survive on, and if you are not willing to go full frugal, figure the things that you want the most. Prioritize them even if they look unimportant to others.

Now that you have thought about the subject, here are seven steps to making a budget.

STEP 1 – Put your financial papers in order. Try to find as much information as possible to make a monthly average of spending. These include all your financial statements like:

- Utility bills (electric, water, etc.)
- Bank statements (deposits and withdrawals)
- Investment accounts (deposits and withdrawals)
- W-2s and paystub
- 1099s
- Credit card bill
- Purchase receipts from the last three months
- Loan and mortgage statements

STEP 2 – Now, you need to find out your income. It could be a regular salary you receive from work or money you get from freelance work. If you receive money from child support or social security, add them to the list as well. If you are self-employed or a freelancer, then use the number from the lowest earned month.

STEP 3 – Now, list your expenses. Take help from the papers you gathered in step one to accurately identify your spending list. This should include:

- Rent or mortgage
- Car loan payments
- Food (groceries and restaurant visits)
- Bills (electricity, water, sewer)
- Insurance payments
- Entertainment
- Travel
- Child care (if you are taking care of someone, all their expenses should also be written)
- Student loan payments
- Personal products
- Savings

Tip: You need to be honest about your buying habits to make a realistic budget; otherwise, you will not follow through with it.

STEP 4 – Now, you need to figure out your fixed expenses. Fixed expenses are the payments that have a fixed value every month. These include:

- Rent or mortgage
- Car loan payments
- Regular child care expenses
- Trash pick up
- If you have a fixed internet fee, then it should be on this list
- If you have the same credit card payments for each month for essential spending, it should be on this list
- If you have to pay a fixed amount and pay a debt using a fixed amount, add savings and debt repayment here as well

STEP 5 – Consequently, determine your variable expenses. These are amounts that change every month. Use your gathered receipts to figure out an estimate for each item on the list. It includes:

- Gas
- Food
- Entertainment
- Gifts
- Travel
- Personal products etc.

STEP 6 – Now, subtract your expenses from the total income amount. In this way, you will have two scenarios.

You will be either left with a positive number which means your income is higher than your expenses. As a result, you can direct some extra cash towards investment and investment accounts like a retirement fund. Or, you will have a negative number which means your expenses are more than your income. This is a sign of change and the fact you need to control spending.

STEP 7 – Lastly, you need to make adjustments to it. If the number you got was negative in the last step, then you can take many steps to make it a positive. This can be done by:

- Spending less, for example, eating out less or spending less on personal products, e.g., clothes, make-up, etc.
- Cutting a category altogether like a gym membership or a club membership
- Earning more either by getting a side job or asking for support from parents etc.
- Reducing your tax burden. Adopting certain tax strategies can increase wealth significantly
- Selling items that are no longer used or wanted

You have made a successful budget if the income and expenses column both have the same amount and are equal. This means that you know where your money is going, and you are adhering to a specific saving goal.

I have made a budget, now what?!

Now, you have numbers to compare and follow through to. Every time you purchase something or give a payment, record it. Monitor and track your expenses in all categories to remain within the value and not surpass it.

To help you only spend your money on mindful items, ask these three questions:

- Do I "really" need it?
- Will it help me, or is it only going to give me momentary happiness?
- Is this purchase supports my system of spending, or is it a bad habit, e.g., junk food or impulse buying?

You will be more motivated towards your budget if you see it every day. You can write them and stick them on the fridge or pin it in your calendar that you often see. Talk about it with your friends, family members, and colleagues. It should be ingrained in your lifestyle and feel natural.

Tip: For making a budget, use spreadsheets for budgeting apps, for they can be regularly updated and accessed anywhere.

Remember, your budget works for you, not you for it. If you have changes in priorities in life like having a child/pet or changing jobs, adjust your budget accordingly. Make sure your budget is helping you to fulfill your financial goals at the time.

Tip: For people who have problematic spending habits and cannot follow through with a budget, they can seek help by adopting an envelope system for a few months. Rather than assigning money, physically place the budgeted amount in envelopes labeled according to expense categories. Then, when you spend, you feel money draining out and stop automatically when it becomes empty.

If you are an impulse buyer or have any other spending problem, a budget can help you identify that. You can then take steps to improve these problems. For example, suppose you update your records every day by sparing one or two minutes. In that case, this budget will prevent you from overspending. Your goal is to keep your expenses lower or equal to your income. If you have extra cash at the end, prioritize savings and investment.

Build Wealth for Investing with Budgeting

Building wealth is the most important thing you can do for your future self. Investing and setting money aside, especially for investing, is one way to ensure that. But, unfortunately, this is seen as an afterthought, and after people have made their expenses, they think about investing.

Investing should be treated as a fixed expense in your budget, and you should prioritize it in your life if you have not already. Of course, if you do not include investment savings in your budget and do not assign any money to it, you will not have any money for investing.

Do not leave one of the most important ways of building wealth on chance and consciously take matters into your own hands. Here are four ways you can do it:

- Invest as a priority
- Assign a budget to investment categories

- Make a comfortable room for investing in your budget
- Figure out waste in your budget

Invest As a Priority

After the month has passed and most of your money is gone, do not think about investing. Following this method will never allow you to invest comfortably and always give you anxiety. Do not decide at the end of the month but rather commit to it at the start and save for it.

Maybe you are not motivated enough, and you are delaying or procrastinating. To help you think and visualize what your investment savings and investment can become in the long run. Many people want to retire early, maybe even you. To ensure that happens, open up a tax-advantaged retirement account or, better yet, start investing in mutual funds. Review every month how much is going into investing from your salary and know that it will become a significant contribution towards your goal.

Another way to motivate yourself is to think of investment to improve your future without much chore or hindrance in your current lifestyle. You can live a financially secure life when you grow older if you just control impulse buying and spend mindfully.

Assign A Budget to Investment Categories

Now, you have found the motivation to invest as a priority; you need to add investment categories in your budget and allot a certain amount of money to it. Treat these categories as you would bill or rent payments. Do not push them at the bottom or forget about them.

Before setting amounts for personal items, food, and entertainment in the variable expenses section, consider putting money in an investment account (if you do not already have one). Even if you thought about using the money in the account for doing a specific thing, e.g., buying a house, label it investing.

Make A Comfortable Room for Investing in Your Budget

When you decide to add a new category in your budget, such as different investment accounts, you will have to reduce some amount from other items on the list. For example, maybe you can reduce your clothing and restaurant spending or eliminate eating outside altogether. The way to move money towards your savings account will depend on your priorities.

Another popular method preached online is 50-30-20. Using this method, 50% of your after-tax income goes to necessary spending like a house, food, etc.; 30% goes to discretionary spending, and the rest 20% is allotted to investing. However, this method should be avoided as you can get confused about your spending numbers and may overspend as a result.

Figure Out Waste in Your Budget

As you make your budget, you will identify wasteful spending almost immediately. Even at one point I had spent a lot of money on things that I did not need or wanted.

To add more money to investment categories comfortably, you can identify and resolve these wasteful expenses. When you are honest and recognize what you are doing is not right, you can remove the problems. These may be subscriptions that you do not use or use very little, habit spending, excessive junk food shopping, etc. Once you have figured them out, redirect them into your investment accounts.

Tell yourself that you do not have enough money to invest is the easy way to get out of a problem. By putting off wasting money today, you will be building yourself a secure future tomorrow.

Chapter 2 – Where Do We Go from Here?

Following the methods from the previous chapter, you will have some modest amount saved up. In a couple of months, you will be ready to do some serious investing.

Before you start to look for schemes, accounts, and plans, you need to figure out your needs. There are many investment options you can choose from. It all depends on your goals. Do you want the safest route to investment, or are you willing to take risks for higher returns? Are you seeking fast gains for a short period, or are you in this for the long haul? Answering these questions can help you identify the investment option suited for you.

Short Term Investments

For a first-time investor, you might be looking for a safe place to put your money before you can use it shortly. Short-term investments are a way to increase the returns of your invested money so you have that cash shortly. However, you will get less safety from them. They are riskier because they have less time to follow the market trend and are subjected to fluctuations in the market.

What Are Short-Term Investments?

These investments you apply for when you need to make money in 3 years or less. You have less safety in protecting your capital, but you will be getting greater returns.

If you have sought advice from others, they may have suggested stocks as an investment option. Not many people know what they are, even if it is seen as a common word. If you want to get big returns on your investment, you should look into methods like buying stocks. They are volatile or riskier but given a bigger period, they generate a good amount of money. They are not good as a short-term investment.

The biggest advantage of investing in a short-term investment plan is that they are highly liquid and one of the safest options out there. You can take out your money whenever you want, and they have very low disadvantages.

Some of the most popular short-term investments are:

- Savings account
- Short term corporate bonds funds
- Money market account
- Cash management accounts
- Short term US government bond fund
- Certificates of deposit
- Treasury

Ultra Short-Term Mutual Fund

These are debt schemes that mature or grow within six months. You will invest in a fixed amount of generating instruments, and they will give you returns very quickly. They are safer to invest in compared to other mutual funds because of the short maturity period. Less time means fewer fluctuations in the interest rate. However, their value rises when the interest rate drops so it is suitable for a falling interest rate scenario.

They are riskier than other liquid funds but give a return of 7-9% on average, which is far more than liquid funds can offer. Even if the funds mostly consist of fixed-income funds, returns are not guaranteed and you can end up with a bad credit score if your manager puts low-quality bonds in your portfolio.

Short Duration Funds

They are debt funds that use debt and money market assets which last for 2-3 years.

How Do Short Duration Funds Work?

Duration: The time denotes how much the interest rate changes. A longer period means higher changes and uncertainty of the fund's value. That is why long-maturity bonds are at more risk than short-maturity ones.

Investments: They invest in many debt securities like corporate bonds, government assets, money market assets, etc. A diverse range maintains liquidity as well.

Earning: As most of the fund's portfolio is made up of debt securities, interest payments will bring profit. When the interest rate decreases, the value of the bonds increases, and it results in capital gains. Similarly, if the opposite happens, the capital loss will be seen. The longer the time, the more capital gain or loss you will get.

Generating Income: There are times when the market is rising and times when it is declining. When markets rise, funds gain higher interest rates, and by changing to short-term securities, they reduce capital loss. Then, when the market is declining, they switch to long-term debt and gain capital. They generate income for a short period.

Risks: They have a moderate interest rate, but they give a higher return than liquid funds for the risk. Some funds are of higher risk than others and can cause you to lose money. Returns are not guaranteed, and the previous performance of funds does not affect its future standings.

How To Spot a Good Performing Short Duration Fund?

They will have three features that will help you identify the fund's performance

Returns: A good-performing fund will go beyond its expected earnings in both benchmark and peer funds. You will need to take account of its progression for the last 3 years.

Risks: First, look at the portfolio. Lower-quality bonds have higher returns but are very risky; the debt payer may not fulfill the payment. Higher-quality bonds carry less credit risk but give lower returns. If you prefer security, then this choice is for you.

Second, it should have a duration that does not maximize interest rate risk. Thirdly, the fund manager or house should choose the best funds for you to invest in.

Note: In mutual funds, you need to track the expense ratio, which is a few you give every year to maintain your fund portfolio. Check if it does not go too high that your returns get overlooked.

Now, you know what options there are available for short-term investments. This might appeal to you because most people want the full safety of their money and guaranteed returns. That is why liquid funds, fixed deposits (FD), and recurring deposits are chosen most by average investors. Sadly, mutual funds did not receive the same love.

Assessing Fears

Many people shy away from investing in mutual funds because they think it is not a safe investment option and does not guarantee returns. You might be fearing the same things. However, mutual funds can give you a lot higher returns on your capital with small risks. If you invest with a set of goals and risks in mind, you can greatly benefit from it.

Three questions build fear:

- Will the company in which you have invested run away with the money?
- Will my money disappear?
- Will I get returns, or all this work will become useless?

First, mutual funds are safe, and no one is going to run away with the money. Mutual fund companies are regulated and supervised, and no fund house can rip you off. A fund house will have a license similar to what a bank has, so they are as secure as banks.

Secondly, a mutual fund's entire purpose is to provide a new earning platform. Any investment that guarantees security gives low yields and is not a good investment opportunity.

They are the best choice because not only do they give inflation-beating returns, but they are tax-efficient, which saves up more money.

If you invest for a longer period, your returns will increase because of compounding effects. The risks can be managed by diversifying your portfolio, maintaining your goals and investing according to them, picking a suitable duration, and assessing risk tolerance. So, do not hesitate to invest for the long haul.

Mindset For Investing in Mutual Funds

When investing, two emotions take control of us and make us emotional. They are "Greed" and "Fear." If you let these two emotions drive you, then you will make worse and worse decisions over time.

You have to be unemotional and follow core values and discipline when investing. You will never be completely perfect in your decisions, and sometimes some emotions will seep in, but you have to control them as much as possible.

There is not only the risk of losing money; there is a risk of missing opportunities. If you mitigate one, the other haunts you. Understand that you will never be risk-free, but you can stop letting that be a burden that weighs heavily on you.

Large Growth Funds

These are portfolios that comprise big company assets and are expected to grow more than average large-cap stocks. Portfolios only focus on the top 70% of expanding industries.

Some best large growth funds are:

- Principal Blue Chip Fund
- Zevenbergen Growth Fund
- Fidelity Blue Chip Growth K6 Fund
- Fidelity Advisor Series Equity Gr Fund
- Lord Abbett Growth Leaders Fund
- T. Rowe Price Lrg Cp Gr
- Morgan Stanley Inst Growth Port

Average Returns on Mutual funds

When a fund catches your eye, you have to see the average return of the said investment first.

What to keep an eye on

- Monitor and assess short term vs. long term gains:

  Stocks are prone to fluctuate in value but given a long time, as a long-term investment, it remains stable. A long-term mutual fund needs to have a 3-5 years record of good performance. Sometimes a mutual fund has a great record but poor management of portfolios. You have to figure out if the current management is the reason for funds' success or just some other reason. A long record means that the strategy being used is working successfully, and it can adjust with market fluctuations.

- Set a good benchmark:

  Index-based or actively managed funds, all types of mutual funds need to have benchmarks that give a clear understanding of average returns. Here are some examples for a few categories:

  - For equities, use S&P 500
  - Russell 1000 and S&P 500 value for large-cap
  - S&P 600 for mid-cap
  - Russell 2000 for small-cap stock
  - Bloomberg Barclays US Aggregate Bond Index for fixed income investment

  In each category of mutual funds, management looks at trends and styles but often, short-term fads do not do well in the future. That is why you should always have a diversified portfolio.

- Have a lookout for fees:

  Fees often overtake your gains in mutual investment, so you have to monitor them. You cannot control market fluctuations or interest rates, but you can choose how much to pay for funds. Fees and expense ratios have been significantly reduced, but you still need to keep an eye for it. To calculate your returns, minus the value of fees from the performance of the fund. The charges vary as well. A large-cap fund with a lot of money will have lower fees, but a short-cap fund with lower amounts will have higher fees. In a fixed income mutual fund, sometimes fees almost take up half the reruns you would get.

- Note your investment patterns:

  Most investors underperform the market because they are following the trend at extremes. They buy and sell at the wrong times because of fear and greed. If you find yourself underperforming in the market, you need to change your buying and selling patterns and learn from your mistakes.

  The best way to see the long performance of the fund, be careful of fees and stand by the funds you choose through fluctuations in the market.

How Can You Evaluate Average Returns?

Previous Performance

Mutual funds have been performing better, almost double the rate, than in the past 15 years. Among the 7 categories of mutual funds, US large-cap stock is the best performing, and short-term bond funds are the worst. Short-term investments cannot be assessed by looking at the past; even 15 years of data is not a predictor of future trends.

Have A Benchmark

There are many mutual funds to choose from, so to pick the best, you need to compare them with their benchmark. Like for large-cap stock mutual funds, compare it to S&P 500.

A benchmark can also be a fund category's average performance. For example, a large-cap stock fund of long-term growth can fall in the category of Large Growth Fund. This method takes into account expense ratios, so it gives a more realistic image.

Compare With Its Category

You cannot track all of your funds, so it is better to only track their category. They can be categorized by stocks, bonds, or any other assets. Each asset can have subcategories like large-cap, mid-cap, etc. It can also be organized as a business sector, like technology.

Mutual Funds Vs. Other Investments

Even only using long-term investments, mutual funds have been shown to grow more than the inflation rate and beat investment returns of other investments like CDs, gold, and treasury bonds.

The CD rate, on average, has been only 2% for an entire decade. Treasuries have a little more than 2% returns, and gold has a little more than 3%. Mutual funds also beat real estate investments which give 4.8% returns. Even if a mutual fund performs below average, it is still giving almost 9% return annually.

Chapter 3 – Mutual Funds: What Are They, Why Do I Want them?

Now, you have some idea about investing in mutual funds, but that is not enough to get comfortable with the concept. Only after you thoroughly understand what they are and how they work will you be able to invest money without worrying too much.

A regular investor thinks of mutual funds as an easy, diversified form of investment that does not require a lot of cash. Instead, the fund gathers money from the investors and buys different stocks, bonds, and other securities.

Mutual Fund 101

It is a metaphorical vehicle for the money. The money goes to buy stocks, bonds, and other assets gathered from thousands of investors. Second, they are managed by money managers that buy the assets in a way that makes money for the investor. Finally, the portfolio is maintained in a way that matches the investment goals.

The investor can have very little money or a large amount of investment in the same fund. This allows regular people to gain professionally managed portfolios of assets. Of course, the more money you have invested, the more you can lose or gain. How a mutual fund is doing is determined by tracking the market cap of the fund.

Fact: Market cap is the value of shares of stock of the fund.

A mutual fund's value is determined by the performance of the assets bought. You can think of it as buying a part of its portfolio's performance or value (a portfolio is a collection of assets and financial investments). It is different from investing in stocks. One share in one mutual fund contains many stocks (and other assets) and not only one. For example, one stock share will be exposed to the performance of Company X, so if Company X goes down, all of the share value as well. On the other hand, a mutual fund share will contain many more business stocks, including Company X. So, if Company X goes down, it will not incur as much losses as it would in the first scenario.

Fact: Outstanding shares are owned by shareholders, institutional investors, or insiders/company's officers).

Each trading day, a mutual funds price or NAV is set and does not rise or fall during the market hours, which falls between 9 A.M. to 5 P.M. EST. One mutual fund portfolio has hundreds of assets and securities attached to it, diversifying investments and reducing risks. Diversification

45

is to spread and buy various different investments, so any harm from any one type is limited. It is important because you do not lose money if one company does bad and keep your money safe. Even big companies go through bad quarters, so sometimes they lose money too.

How Do Mutual Funds Work?

Think of a mutual fund as a company, and you buy its assets and partial ownership. It is an investment and an actual company, the difference being that it does not make any products. Instead, it is a business of making investments. You earn money through three methods

- Dividends from stock and interest on bonds become a source of income generation. During distribution, a fund pays its investors this income yearly. You can reinvest or take the money; it is your choice.

  Fact: Dividends is money or bonus a company gives to the shareholders on different occasions, for example, a company has reached their goal.

- The securities or assets sold at a higher price than when they were bought give a capital gain to you. In distribution, you can receive this gain, but some funds may not do that.

46

- If fund holdings reach a higher price than they were previously and they are in your portfolio, you can sell them to make a profit.

A fund manager or investment advisor works to make as much profit as he can for the shareholders. They, sometimes, are themselves, owners of funds, as well. The fund manager can have an analyst working with him to determine the best funds. A fund accountant daily calculates the value of the funds, and a compliance officer or lawyer works out government regulations affecting their work. Many mutual funds are a part of a large investment organization, including Fidelity Investments, The Vanguard Group, and Oppenheimer.

When Are Mutual Funds Beneficial?

You can start your investing journey by buying some individual stocks on your own into your portfolio. Then, if you have time for researching, the only expenses you will pay are transaction fees.

You can start by buying stocks of high-quality companies like Target, Microsoft, etc. They can be the first picks of your diversified portfolio. Always see that the expense ratio is low; around 1% is advised. The cost is very important when buying a mutual fund, but every mutual fund cost varies according to its type. You will need to know how much money you need to save up before you start investing in different investment types.

Different Types of Mutual Funds

You may have an idea now of what you want your investments to do and what your goals are. Whether you want to park your money for a while before purchasing a car or you want to invest till retirement. Depending on your decisions, you will have to develop a strategy of buying ultra-short-term funds, short-term funds, and long-term funds. However, these are only one way to differentiate different funds in mutual funds.

There are categories of mutual funds, which are divided based on the securities they provide. Thus, there is a type for every investor and every investor strategy.

Fact: Securities are financial instruments or assets that are traded in the financial market.

By learning the information down below, you will be getting a better understanding of different types of funds and their effects on your goals in the future. You will be able to make better decisions and be on the right track to success.

Equity Fund

These are also called stock funds and take up the largest part of the fund. This fund invests mainly in stocks. There are various subcategories within this type as well.

They are divided by the company size they invest in – Small-cap (capitalization), Mid-cap, Large-cap. They are also divided by aggressive growth, income-oriented, and value. They can be domestic funds or foreign funds.

Fact: Value fund is a strategy that comprises investing in low growth but high-quality stocks that have low market prices.

A fund is in a particular company size category and also an approaching category. For example, high-growth funds do not give dividends but give a lot more annual return. This means you have more interest returns, and more money is generated. A mix of value and growth funds is an investment blend, a combination of both to get benefits of both funds. Companies that are neither growth nor value funds are in this category.

Mutual fund portfolios follow a strategy that will mix different approaches and sizes of companies. This is to minimize the risks by increasing diversity. An example of this can be a large-cap company whose prices have decreased and can be in the category of large-cap value fund. Another example is a fund in a new technology company just starting its business that would go in a small-cap growth fund category.

Fixed Income Fund

These are also called bond funds. These funds pay the investor a set rate of interest or return by investing in government bonds, corporate bonds, etc. The portfolio is made up of assets that generate interests for investors.

There are various types of bond funds, and each carries a different yield potential or how much money/return they can generate. These funds are usually bought at a lower price to be later sold at a profit. These generate more money than certificates of deposit; however, they are riskier. For instance, high yield junk bonds are riskier than bond funds that have government assets. Also, if the rate of interest rises, the value of the fund decreases.

Fact: Yield is the income return or extra money generated by investments and different types of assets. This includes the interests and dividends that you will receive.

Index Fund

Indexes have become popular in recent years. Index fund tries to copy the results of the market, which has grown over the years. People investing in these funds believe that it is not possible to beat the market consistently. The manager purchases funds in the major market in indexes like DJIA (Dow Jones Industrial Average). These are low-yield but are cost-friendly and do not require an advisor or high fees to set up.

Balanced Fund

These are also called asset allocation funds. These funds' objective is to diversify the assets and build a portfolio made up of stocks, bonds, money market assets, and other types of assets.

There are two strategies to go about these funds. One is that funds follow a fixed allocation strategy which is predictable. Second is the dynamic allocation of funds in which your (the investor) goals are met. The changes are related to the market, business, and your goal changes. In a dynamic fund, the percentages and ratio of asset types can be changed freely by the manager.

Money Market Funds

They are made with risk-free debt securities, which are short-term. These give out more than regular savings accounts but less than CDs (certificate of deposit). They are at risk-free; however, in the 2008 financial crisis, these funds did experience a loss. They are risk-free because they only invest in assets that mature in less time, commonly in 1 year. It is suitable for people who want to grow wealth quickly and need the money in the near future, like buying a house.

Income Funds

People wanting to generate income through investment mainly invest in these funds, which is a popular choice. They give a steady rate of money to you. The funds invest in high yield corporate bonds, and you have it till it reaches maturity. A maturity date is written in the bond's prospectus and sometimes with its name as well; for example, "One-year fixed-rate bond." With interest being paid on them, you will receive a steady income flow. However, they are not the best way to minimize taxes. You will learn about taxes and fees in upcoming chapters.

Global Funds

Do not confuse this with international funds that invest in stocks and other assets outside your country. Global funds can invest in foreign and domestic funds. However, they are riskier and are subject to political risks. Many countries may outperform your own country's economy, so it is wise to have some in your portfolio. Also, it can help make a much more diversified portfolio which will save some money if your home country has gone through a financial crisis.

Specialty Funds

These funds are nearly placed in other categories but are very popular and have proven to have growth potential. However, these funds lack diversity and focus on the part of the economy. For example, sector funds target specific industries like technology or health. These are much riskier (as they are less diverse) but have the potential for large gains.

Another type is regional funds that differentiate the funds according to areas. These areas can comprise one or multiple countries. Again, they have a lot more risks but the potential for higher yields.

Ethical funds are funds directed to only those companies that follow certain ethics or beliefs. For example, an investor does not want to invest in the tobacco, alcohol, and weapons industry. Another example would be to buy funds from companies that are helping the green cause. That idea has come from making good money while also maintaining a good conscience and being responsible for your money.

Other types of mutual funds are sector funds, alternative funds, smart-beta funds, and mutual funds that buy other mutual funds. The problem is that there are hundreds of mutual funds to choose from, and you can make money using hundreds of different strategies.

Exchange-Traded Funds or ETFs

This type of investment is becoming popular in recent years as well. They are mutual funds but built as investment trusts which deal like stocks and carry benefits of the stock exchange. They have low costs; they can be traded at any time of a trading day and can be sold short and bought as well. They are more liquid than other types of mutual funds and save you from taxes in the future.

Benefits of EFTs

They are a type of mutual fund that carries many advantages over other mutual fund types. The four most important benefits it gives are:

Flexibility in trade

Normally, mutual funds are traded once per day, and it is convenient to not think about market fluctuations, but if you want more flexibility and you are investing in short-term funds, then this might be a problem.

EFTs work like stock and are traded during hours when markets are open. Share prices change, and investors know how much they paid and sold the funds within moments rather than waiting for the day to end. Intraday management of portfolios becomes very easy and quick. It is far easier to sell and buy assets as well.

EFT investors can make quicker, more timely choices and have many different ways of purchasing. They can also be bought on margin by a broker lending cash to you. Short selling can also be done effectively.

Fact: Short selling means you can borrow assets from the firm you work with and sell those assets at the same time. The strategy is that you will wait for its prices to go down, and then you buy them back at a lower price, which leaves you with a profit.

More diverse funds

You may want to invest in various funds and stocks but lack the knowledge to do so. You are not exposed to different sectors, industries, or regions, but EFT provides that exposure.

You can trade anywhere, using any currency. You can trade in the highest-yielding currencies and make even more returns. Sometimes you can see potential losses in one sector and also are limited to diversify because of taxes. If this occurs, then you can buy EFTs that shorts the industry.

To help you get started, these are the steps you should take.

1. Think about your goals for mutual investment

    If you are saving up your son's tuition or a good retirement, a long-term investment is a good choice.

    If you want to buy a house or a vehicle, e.g., a car soon, think about a money market mutual fund or government bond fund. However, you need the money to be as safe as possible in this situation, so consider a high interest giving account and deposit account. Because they are insured, you will not lose money.

2. Choose the mutual fund right for you

    Goals will define what strategies you are going to follow to build your portfolio. The strategies will help you choose the funds.

In long-term funds, your money will be in investing for 20-30 years. In this scenario, you should place the majority of it in stock-based mutual funds, around 100%. Choose funds that are marked as "growth funds." These marks indicate businesses that will grow quicker. They have risks but also have high yields. These funds include " VIGAX" Vanguard Growth Index Fund and "FDSVX" Fidelity Growth Discovery Fund.

In short-term funds, reduce your risks as much as possible, so you have money when you need it. Invest majority in bond funds and rest in stocks, almost 30%. This will provide you with income generation through bonds and stocks that can grow, will make a lot of money. Income-generating funds include "PTTAX" or PIMCO total return and "VEIPX" or Vanguard Equity Income Fund.

In mid-term funds, invest both in stocks and bonds equally. This will give you a higher chance of rapid growth. Balanced mutual funds include "VWINX" or Vanguard Wellesley Income Fund and ABALX or American Funds American Balanced fund.

You can skip picking a portfolio allocation and choose a target-date fund. In this, you can withdraw your fund in the year specified by the target date and also allocate your assets, bonds, and equities. First, it will invest in riskier, higher-yielding assets and then switch to lower-risk assets as the date nears.

Benefits of Mutual Funds

Mutual funds are the most popular way to invest today, and there are many reasons why:

High-quality fund management

Purchasing a mutual fund comes with a management fee that will be a part of your expense ratio. This money is used to pay a manager that will trade assets for you with their expertise. In addition, you can get professional help to manage portfolios at a good price.

Dividends can be invested again

You have invested a modest amount and found some dividends at the end of the year. Now, you can use these dividends and other interest income to buy more mutual funds without you opening the wallet. It will become a money-generating cycle that will help you grow your wealth.

Low risks

Mutual funds are a very diversified form of investing that invests in different assets with 50-500. A lot of stock index mutual funds own more than a thousand individual stocks. This reduces the chances of you losing your originally invested money or principal money. If you are a conservative investor, this is what you want.

Cost-effective and convenient

Unlike other forms of investing, mutual funds give a good amount of yield without much learning. They are easy to get into and not difficult to buy or understand. They can be invested by you using a modest amount of money, as low as $2500. They are traded only once a day.

The advantages of mutual funds are recognized by investors around the world. By understanding them, you are on the right track to investing in them yourself. Continue reading to unlock more information about smartly getting into investment so that you make a lot more money in the future.

Chapter 4 – Mutual Funds That Are Right for Me

New-time investors should be smart and be aware of their goals and objectives. They should prepare for a long-term strategy accordingly. If you want to get into mutual funds and start investing yourself without using professional services, then you should be knowledgeable about the best kinds of low-cost funds available. You can then choose what funds you want from there.

What to Consider When Buying a Mutual Fund?

Here is some advice on purchasing mutual funds by yourself so that your choices are meaningful and profitable.

- Consider no-load funds
  If you want to start your investing journey with mutual funds alone, you should start by purchasing no-load funds. Without extra charges of brokers and sales, these funds are a great way for a new investor to enter mutual funds. Moreover, over a long period of time, no-load funds have given more returns to their investors than load funds. If your goal is to have a comfortable retirement and are willing to do

the purchasing and holding of the funds yourself, this option best suits you.

- Use best fund companies
  If you are planning to invest in mutual funds for a long time, chances are that your financial goals are also long-term. It is, therefore, very critical to be knowledgeable about the best no-load mutual fund companies that you can invest through. The companies should also provide a large list of mutual fund categories to choose from so your portfolio can become diversified. Here are some of the best no-load mutual fund companies you can work with:
  - Vanguard Investment
  - Fidelity
  - T. Rowe Price

- Look at Index fund
  An example of it is the S&P 500. Index funds are a good starting point for building a diversified portfolio of your mutual funds. Just one fund can expose you to hundreds of different stocks that belong to different companies and also various industries. They also have a very low expense ratio. Your primary goal of building a diversified, low-cost mutual fund portfolio will be on track with them. Some mutual fund companies that sell index funds are:
  - Vanguard Investment

- Fidelity
- T. Rowe Price
- Charles Schwab

Target Date Mutual Funds

They are funds that are good choices for people investing till a specific year. It will include a mixture of stocks, bonds, and cash to invest in. When the time of maturation arises, the fund manager or the investors themselves switch out stocks for bonds and other short-term investments. This way, you can just sit back and see the investment grow your wealth without much effort. If you want to retire by 2040, search for a target fund in the company of your choice for that date and then buy it. Then, you only have to do yearly research and add new investment money to it while living your best life.

How To Make a Portfolio?

You need to have an idea of building a successful portfolio before buying any funds.

- You need to understand your goals and develop a strategy according to those goals. Have a blueprint of your investment plan in your mind, and it is beneficial to even write it on your computer so you can access and change it as well. You have to clear your long-term plans, what big purchases you want to do and when you want to retire.

- You need to keep everything simple and avoid complications in your portfolio. For example, do not try a strategy or buy a fund that you do not understand.

- Be sure to not overthink and overanalyze. When you get started, you will start learning. If you wait too long, you might miss an opportunity and undermine your goals.

What Is Special About the Exchange Trade Fund (ETF)?

ETFs (Exchange Traded Funds) are very interesting, diverse, and beneficial mutual funds that you cannot ignore. Exchange-traded funds are a mixture of all kinds of mutual funds, open and close-ended. They hold various assets, commodities, bonds, and stocks. They can be traded in real-time. They trade near their asset value as well. If you are trading in mutual funds, you need to have a good understanding of them.

Fact: Close-ended funds have a specific amount of shares that a company offers for investors to buy, while open-ended funds have companies sell shares for investors to purchase.

Further advantages of ETF are:

- More Liquidity
  This is important for investors wanting more access to their money. ETF trades do not need to wait for the day to end but can be traded anytime during market hours.

- Targeting sectors
  You can buy an ETF, you can choose a segment of the economy your funds will belong to. This way, you can get a fund from a segment, e.g., health, that you did not have any exposure to previously. You can also increase the diversity of your portfolio.

- Starting small is easy
  ETFs behave like stocks, so you can buy small positions of them and take advantage of position sizing. There is no minimum on how much you need to invest. You can take a position in a specific ETF of your liking.

  Fact: Position is the amount of an asset, security, or property owned by an investor.

- More investment choices
  They can open new investment opportunities in alternative or exotic investment choices that are not open for new investors. New products introduce EFT commodities fairly often.

The downsides:

Nothing can be perfect, and this is true for mutual funds as well. There are numerous benefits of this type of fund. Still, to maximize returns on it, you need to understand two very critical downsides of it. These are:

- Over diversification
  Exchange traded funds (EFT) are, most of the time, not actively managed funds, so it is possible that they may contain a lot of bad quality stocks and other assets. It is better to buy a diverse range of stocks in good companies with great expected growths and performance rather than to buy the entire index of companies, good and bad ones.

- Problems in rebalancing
  As mentioned before, ETFs are not actively managed most of the time and do not rebalance their portfolios. As time passes, some companies in

the index grow a lot, and they increase in price and become a larger part of the index. Some company's stock prices go down, and they become a smaller slice in the index. ETF tracks the index and follows it, so you can end up with more expensive stocks than lower, valued stocks over time.

How to steer the disadvantages?

These downfalls can be avoided if you have full knowledge of them and have taken measures to ensure that an ETF does you more good than harm. If you buy ETFs alongside individual stocks, then its disadvantages will go away. Individual stocks will decrease the harm done by bad quality stocks in ETFs and help in rebalancing (as they can be actively managed). There are times when ETFs will benefit you and times when it will be smart to buy stocks individually. You can start mutual fund investing by using ETFs and then adding individual stocks when your portfolio reaches a certain amount, for example, $30,000. They are extremely beneficial for beginners. It can add useful diversification in portfolios for small investors and add specific diversity for larger investors.

Load and No-Load Funds

Mutual funds are a business that involves a lot of money going in and out of companies and individuals. There are hundreds of classes of mutual fund types and hundreds of products and commodities to invest in, so it is important that we choose wisely. Your choice will depend upon your goals, type, size, etc.

One of the most important aspects when buying a mutual fund is the cost. There are two types of mutual funds that are related to cost. Load and no-load mutual funds.

Load Funds

Load funds are a type of mutual fund that has more expenses attached to them. It is called a commission or a sales charge. The charges are termed as loads. A fund manager, broker, or investment advisor charges this money for their services and expert opinions. A fund manager will also want to take full control of your money for a substantial amount of time, and they advise against hedging and trading funds.

Fact: Hedging is a strategy to decrease risks in investing; normally, it is done by taking an opposite position in a security.

Pros

Load funds are costly, but they do have some benefits:

- Professional Advice
  The services include processing different transactions, but the most important aspect is the advice you will get. These advisors claim to identify and choose the best-performing mutual funds for you.
  Professionals and advisors offering these services have great knowledge of the financial markets. They have an eye on recent developments and even know insights and information that have not hit the news yet. They have data on the best and the worst-performing funds. You, by yourself, may not have the professional insights and are not able to pick the best possible mutual funds right for you.

- Mindful decisions
  The advice also comes with the professionals helping and educating you on making the best decisions. The advisors or managers can provide you with the necessary research and analysis and present them to you. You can now make your own decisions based on the reports given. You will feel more secure in your choices and feel more motivated.

You need to check if the advisors or managers that are working for you are actually worth your dollars or not. Their decision is based on their competence, so you need to make the best choice when picking your advisor. You will also need to check the numbers given in the report that your advisor sends you. Finally, you have to make sure everything is correct and add up before investing.

Cons

The main disadvantage, which is enough to deter swarms of investors away, is cost. Load funds have loads on them, meaning more expenses from commission and sales charges. They can get very high if you are not careful about choosing them. They can use up the money that you can instead park in an investment plan. For example, if you are purchasing a fund that is $5000 with a 10% load, the invested money will actually be $4500.

The load can be paid in three ways which give flexibility to the buyer. These are:
- Upfront payment.
- Payment is given at the end of a transaction.
- Payment under a designated period for all the annual loads.

The share class can also affect the amount of load and the time of payment of that load.

When Is It Beneficial?

The most important aspect when buying a load fund is the worth of the fund and its performance. Every fund has a benchmark, and the performance can be judged by the benchmark value as well. Therefore, the new load fund prospectus you are considering purchasing should beat its peers when compared to the index. Costs should also be considered, whether a load fund asks a lot of money or a substantial amount.

Suppose the fund you are thinking about buying is not performing well in the index or not reaching its benchmark. In that case, you should not consider paying a third party to manage it and look at other funds. Many fund managers will say that past performance is not an indicator for the future, but it is a crucial aspect of judging a good mutual fund and decreasing risks. Many sites can give an accurate description of the performance, so you can check the funds worth yourself.

Buying Only One Fund

If you want to take a more conservative and cautious route to mutual funds, you could just buy one mutual fund. However, by choosing the right fund, you can keep costs low and funds diversified.

Balanced funds

These are also called hybrid funds because they have balanced or a mix of different assets such as stocks and bonds. The investments are fixed, and they are bought and sold according to strategic planning. An example of a good balanced fund is (FBALX) Fidelity Balanced Fund which has assets allocated as 68% stock, 30% assets and rests as cash. This kind of distribution is diversified enough to make it a medium-risk investment.

No-Load Funds

The commission and sales charges that are also called loads are not attached to these kinds of funds. They do not come with professional advice, help, or services. Instead, you, the investor, have to buy the funds yourself. Without advice, you need to pick the best option directly from the investment company. There is no advisor service involved, so no need for advisor's charges.

Pros

The most important advantages of this kind of mutual funds are:

- More money for investing
  If there is no money taken away from you, in the form of fees, then that money can be used in various investment opportunities. The growth of your investment will be substantially higher because of the higher capital invested initially. If we continue to discuss the example mentioned earlier of you investing $5000, you will end up with $500 less capital because of the load charge. But, with a no-load fund, you can invest all $5000 and reap the benefits afterward.

- Being safe from fraud
  Mentioned before, a professional advisor is worth the money if they show competence and expertise, but unfortunately, that can be forged, and complete novices can pretend to be advisors only to fall short of your expectations. Some people can have the degrees and experience but lack the cleverness and intuitiveness to pick the best funds.
  Both of these classes of people can take your money and leave you with clueless decisions. When purchasing a no-load fund, you do not need a third party to pay advice for. Also, anyone demanding money from you and promising wealth to you

afterward is usually a scammer who will run away with your cash. Do not give in to greed and buy these people to give you inaccurate recommendations.

Cons

The only disadvantage of no-load funds is:
- No guidance
  You are the only one responsible for transferring money, researching, analyzing, and buying good funds. This is only advised to those who have experience in this industry or are a professional themselves. Otherwise, it is recommended that you do extreme research and analytics yourself.

Creating Your Own Mutual Fund

When you start investing, you will hear long-time investors in mutual funds start to talk about creating their own mutual funds. If you meet the requirements and can pay the start-up money, you can make your own fund.

Requirements

The SEC (Security and Exchange Commission) says that all mutual fund managers must be registered as investment advisors. The laws governing regulatory affairs are different from state to state, so you need to check with an attorney beforehand. They can also help with the paperwork, which is highly complicated. Creating an actual mutual fund is easier than that.

You can also seek help from a company specializing in aiding advisors to make their own funds (sometimes they pay for the start-up fee). To get aid, you need to show your competence and submit a business plan to the company.

Costs

Start-up can cost from $25,000, plus it can be more depending on the type of the mutual fund. Start-ups are not the only expense when creating a mutual fund; there are also incredibly high maintenance expenses. You have to pay for registrations, and you have to register for doing business in each state and all share classes you will offer funds in. You will have to make a brand new investment trust or add more funds to a previous one. You will have expenses of printing prospectus, legal services, etc.

Should You Create Your Own Mutual Fund?

The cost of starting and running the mutual fund is so high that it can be considered prohibitive. After minus-ing the running costs, the net return can be so low that it may seem not worth it. However, if that fund increases in assets, then the fund's price will rise and also its profitability.

Even if you are a registered investment advisor, have the ability to run such a business, and have the amount needed to do so, you should not create a mutual fund without good backing to prove its attractiveness to other investors and the market. Unless you firmly believe that the fund is going to be popular to produce profit, you will be taking a very big risk.

Taking part in mutual funds as an investor will generate steady money with very low risks instead.

Minimum Amounts

Mutual funds are very popular, but they have some high minimums. If you are a beginning investor, you will need to save up a bit before investing. However, some mutual funds can be opened with only $500. The types affect the pricing, so it is beneficial for first-time investors to shop before buying anything. Young investors in their 20s would prefer smaller investing minimums because that is the only option they have with limited savings, and an experienced investor can open small mutual funds to diversify.

Minimums are necessary to keep the mutual funds running and the money entering the investment world. A higher minimum can be associated with higher benefits and returns expectations, but that may not be the case for some. Some do not have a minimum, such as IRAs 401k funds. Even mutual fund companies have minimums; some of the prominent ones are listed below:
- For Vanguard, the minimum is $3,000
- For Fidelity Investments, the minimum is $2,500
- For Charles Schwab, the minimum is $0
- For TD Ameritrade, the minimum is $0

Is Investing in Minimums a Good Decision?

Mutual funds minimums are not specified and can be increased or decreased based on the fund manager's decisions. This means that you can pay less for an investment minimum if the fund manager allows you to. That is why it is important to look and window shop for fund managers and mutual funds so that you can enter the game at a low price. By looking at all the options, you are not forced to pay high upfront minimums when just starting out.

Steps For Setting Up Your First Mutual Investment

Find good mutual funds

You can use websites like Maxfunds, Morningstar, Lipper, etc., to help you get information on different mutual funds in different categories. The categories you choose can be a company of your interest or industry that you already follow. For example, if you like sports, find mutual funds in the category of uniform companies, sport equipment manufacturing, etc. If you are interested in technology, you will be more motivated and informed about the funds' value when you buy mutual funds in the technology industry. Many brokerage sites also offer these services. To help you find what you want, check for:

- Previous Performance: Compare them to similar fund or benchmark values.

- Expenses Ratio: The average rate is about 0.5%, but you can find even lower rates.
- Load Fee: These are your broker's sales commission charges for the fund you bought from them. There are "load" mutual funds that require this fee and "no-load" mutual funds that do not. Try to buy funds that have no load fees.
- Management: Mutual funds are classified into active and passively managed funds. Actively managed to have more potential for growth and beats the benchmark value while passive growth's goal is to reach it. However, passively managed funds are cheaper and grow more than "active" in the long run.

Get an investment account

The purpose of opening an investment account is to allow you to park your money and make decisions regarding the allocation of funds. Using this account, you can buy assets like stocks, bonds, ETFs, etc. Along with it, you will see an increase in return because they can be a long-term investment. If you have retirement accounts, you can still invest in mutual funds using them. However, if you do not have these accounts, then you can open a brokerage account by yourself and invest in:

- IRAs or Individual Retirement Accounts: you can put money in mutual funds for retirement, and no tax will be deducted from them.
- Taxable brokerage accounts: These allow you to take out your money without penalties but lack the tax benefits provided by retirement accounts.
- Education savings accounts: In this, the money here is invested in mutual funds for your child's college.

Fact: A brokerage account is a type of investment account that is mainly opened so that you can purchase and sell assets, including mutual funds. An account can be set up by partnering with a licensed brokerage firm. You will deposit the money, and the brokerage fund will trade on your behalf.

Buy shares of your mutual funds

First, you need to make sure you have enough money for investing, as soon mutual funds have investment minimums. It can be $3000-$10,000, but many individual stocks and EFT (exchange-traded funds) do not have such limits.

Plan your investing future

You do not just need to know how to invest but also how to keep investing. It is not going to be a once-in-a-lifetime activity. The brokerage trader platform, if asked, could make continuous investments in the time frame you specify, weekly or monthly. This way, you will not need to place money in your account again and again for investing. This strategy works well for growing wealth and reducing your chances of buying big when everyone is buying, and the prices are skyrocketing.

Also, continue to check on your investments at least once a year. Check whether the funds you have match your goals and strategy. Rebalancing your portfolio is important, and if you want to skip this step, some companies like Robo advisors offer this service with their management. More details will be discussed in chapter 7.

Have a plan when you want to stop

Like withdrawing your 401k at the time of retirement, you will eventually sell your shares for goals you have set. Here, you will pay fees for mutual funds with back-end loads and also give taxes on capital gains. This is why it is important to minimize tax by talking and taking the advice of tax and financial advisors.

Should You Consider Ultra-Short-Term Mutual Funds?

The advantages of this type of mutual fund are that:

- They are highly liquid and are similar to liquid funds.
- When you dig through your ultra-short-term funds, some can give you high returns. These give more profit when markets are seeing a decrease in interest rates.
- It is the number one choice for those looking to place their money for a short duration to generate profit or dividends.
- They are relatively safe from interest rate risks because they are of such short duration. When the interest rate fluctuates (which happens with time), so does the bond price.
- This is designed to appeal to conservative investors.
- These can be used as a substitute for banks and generate more money.
- By a systematic withdrawal plan, it can generate income.
- You can create an emergency fund as well.

Note: A conservative investor is a person that wants to retain or preserve the value of their investment portfolio. They prioritize saving their money and do not bet on the growth of the market. They take fewer risks.

Disadvantages

- Ultra-short-term mutual funds can be risky to invest in because some schemes have low-rated instruments. Therefore, it is riskier than liquid funds like saving accounts, retirement accounts, etc.
- These funds can make you prone to credit risks.
- If you want guaranteed returns, you may want to look at safer options before investing in ultra-short-term mutual funds.
- To start investing and have great returns at the end, you need full information about all the costs and fees. Without this knowledge, you can lose money, waste time, and become vulnerable to scammers.

How To Analyze Mutual Funds?

You can pick and choose from great mutual funds on different research sites online these days, but you should understand what you want and set features to look for before you begin.

- The first thing you need to look at is the past performance. If a fund has a good record of more than 10 years, then you can consider buying it.

- Not only past performance, but also monitor current market trends.
- Make sure the no-load fund is of low cost or low expense ratio.

Fact: Looking out for the expense ratio for index funds is more important because the fund manager does not want to go beyond the market but match it.

- For actively managed funds, where a fund manager is trying to go beyond the market and make better returns, check if the manager has a good track record of 3-5 years.

Fact: An actively managed fund is where a professional team or person decides where to regularly invest funds. A passively managed fund is not regularly managed by professionals. Actively managed funds have a higher expense ratio than passively managed funds.

Chapter 5 – Fees?! What fees?

Yes, there are places where you have to pay a fee during investing. You need to be very careful about these fees because they can affect your returns greatly. A badly managed portfolio that does not consider expenses and fees will sometimes have 30 to 40% of their profits or returns eaten up by them.

While choosing mutual funds, their costs and fees should be at the top of your prioritized list. Even a short reduction can save you a lot of money.

How are fees deducted? What investors look out for is the expense ratio, also known as the total management expense ratio or (MER). This number is written under "Shareholders fees" in a fund's prospectus, which you will read before purchasing it. This also includes investment management fees.

Mutual funds and ETFs require an investment management fee, which the fund companies adjust themselves without giving regular statements to the investors. The result of the adjustment is seen in NAV (net asset value) which is written as a fixed price. NAV is calculated by subtracting the expense ratio from total returns. You will see the fund's previous NAV values in tracking sheets within bonus documents.

ETF companies also charge manager salaries, custodial devices, and marketing costs as well. These are also deducted from NAV. For example, if you have invested in a $50,000 ETF with a 0.75% annual expense ratio, then you will lose $375 the next year if no returns are gathered that year. Your total will become 49,625.

Example:

Expense ratio of one year = percentage*total value/ 100

= 0.75*50,000/100

=$375

If no returns are gathered, then

Current amount= Total value - expenses ratio

=50,000-375

=$49,625

Fees affect returns a lot more when you are investing for a longer period. This is because fees compound or add up. For instance, if you have invested $100, which grows annually 7%, and has an expense ratio of 1%, you will get $184 in returns for 14 years. Without the expense ratio, the return would have been $198, which means the fee has eaten up almost 10% of your returns.

Example:

Without expenses ratio

*Current amount = Initial investment * Rate of growth * Time/100 + Initial investment*

*= 100 * 7 * 14/100 + 100*

= $198

With expense ratio

Current amount = 198-14 (1% for 14 years)

= $184

The difference = 198-184 = 14

*Percentage of returns lost = 14/198 * 100*

= 8.3% ~ 10%

What Is the Total Cost of an ETF?

The expense ratio is one of the most important fees, but there are trading fees that are for ETFs. In addition, other factors are involved with costs, such as:

- Bid-ask spread: the difference between purchasing and selling cost.
- Commission fees

These two occur only at the time of a transaction.

Bid-ask spread can be calculated by minus-ing the bid from ask, dividing the result by share price, and then multiplying by hundred – *Bid-Ask/share price * 100*

Example:

A stock has a bid price of $9.95, and ask is $10, then

*=9.95-10/10*100*

= 0.5%

There is an easy formula that takes into account expenses ratio, commission fee, and bid-ask spread and gives a yearly fee percent.

- Leave the expense ratio as a percentage
- Calculate the annual bid-ask spread by dividing the bid-ask spread by the holding period, for example, 2 for 2 years holding period.

  Example: 0.05% (from the above example) * 2 (for 2 years holding period) = 0.1%

- Some brokerage services do not charge commission fees. If they do, multiply the commission fee by 2, divide it by the total dollar amount, and multiply again by 100.
- Lastly, add all three amounts to get a yearly fee percent.

The longer you will hold your funds, the lower will be the fee percentage. Moreover, costs like premiums and discounts can also affect this value.

Maintenance Fees and Mutual Funds

Mutual funds maintenance fees are distributed as:

- Annual fund operating expenses: Involves running costs such as workers' salaries, legal expenses, marketing expenses, etc.
- Shareholders fees. A one-time cost such as commission sales charges when you purchase and give away a share.

These are important details written in the prospectus of a mutual fund. In the document you find on the fund's website, you can search for these terms.

Annual Fund Operating Expenses

You cannot avoid these fees, as this is the money that runs the management offices, but they vary in amount, and you can choose the most suitable. The cost annually 0.24% to 1.5% of your returns. Actively managed funds cost higher than passively managed ones.

The costs under this heading will include:

- Management fees
- 12b-1 fees
- Other expenses

This is reflected in NAV.

Shareholders Fees

The fees and expenses involved are:

- Sales load: Extra charges you pay when you purchase and sell shares, often to a third party that introduces you to that share. These are taken as a percentage of the invested amount.
- Redemption fee: Depending on the fund's specified period, if you sell a fund 'shortly' after purchasing it, then this fee is applied.
- Exchange fee: If you transfer a share from one fund to another in the same company, this fee is applied.

- Account fees: These are charged if your balance is lower than a specified amount in your account.
- Purchase fee: When you buy a fund, you also give this fee to the fund.

Brokers sometimes also take transaction charges for purchasing and selling. One transaction can be $10-$75. However, some brokers do not charge any transaction fees, such as E-Trade and Charles Schwab.

Mutual Fund Share Classes in Load Funds

Paying a higher amount on a fund does not guarantee that the fund will do well. On the contrary, a fund manager usually takes more risks with more costly funds. When choosing a mutual fund with loads, you need to avoid giving high fees only to lose your capital. This is why it is important to find which class of share would be suitable for you.

A class of shares will designate the amount, time, and kind of fees you will be charged with. These can be referred to as the ABCs of mutual funds.

A class of shares will impact the amount of your sales load. It is categorized into three types. A company can have more classes, but the three main ones are A, B, and C. They are also called A shares, B shares, and C shares. Each class has its benefits and disadvantages.

- A-Class: These have a front-end sales load of about 2-5%.
- B-Class: These have a back-end sales load, which you do not need to pay before a specified period, often 7 years. They, however, charge higher annual fees than A-class shares.
- C -Class: These have commission charges annually you have the fund.

The difference between the classes gives you the chance to select an appropriate payment method that suits you the most. It is designed to help investors and shows when the amount needs to be paid.

Fact: Back-end sales load is also called "Contingent deferred sales charge" (CDSC) or "Contingent deferred sales load" (CDSL).

The important thing is that during purchasing of a fund, ask the broker or finance professional to explain all the charges you will pay, including to them. A higher-cost mutual fund should give better returns than a lower-cost to generate the same amount of money.

Now, you know that funds come in "load" and "no-load" options. But, there are two types of load funds as well. These are

- Front-end loads

- Back-end loads

As the name suggests, a front-end load is a fee that you pay at the time of purchase, and a back-end load is that you pay when the fund is sold. Thus, class A has front ends loads, and Class B shares have, normally, back-end loads.

Front-End Loads

They are suitable for those who want to invest long-term and also want to purchase many shares.

Pros

Class A shares and funds with front-end loads provide you with discounts that depend on the amount you will invest. Therefore, the more you invest, the more discounts you will receive. These discounts are also called breakpoints. A firm will offer multiple breakpoints in investing amounts so that if you exceed one of them, you could claim a discount associated with it.

You can also get a breakpoint by sending a letter indicating that you, or your family, will purchase more shares shortly. This Is also called "the right of accumulation." These loads should not be higher than 8.5%.

Cons

When you buy a Class A share, your investment amount, in the beginning, is reduced.

Back-End Loads

Pros

If you want to use a smaller amount of money to invest and retain a fund for a long period, this will sound appealing. The sales charges in this category will not cut your initial investment capital, and all of it can go into investing. The load on the fund will decrease over time, and after a certain time, it will completely disappear.

Cons

You need to assess your financial and investment goals before purchasing a fund that comes with a back-end load. These loads are considerably higher than front-end loads or Class A shares. You cannot avail of discounts or breakpoints. If you end up selling the fund prematurely and did not retain it till a particular period, then you would have to pay the sales charges, which will cut your returns significantly. You will need to keep monitoring your back-end shares to know when they become ready to reduce or eliminate sales charges.

Fact: In Class C shares, your back-end load does not disappear over time, but they are lower than Class B share loads.

Taxes and Mutual Funds

When you own and sell mutual funds, you have to pay taxes on them. These include taxes on dividends, earnings, returns, and a capital gain tax when you sell that share. The tax rate varies following various factors, including distribution, period of holding the investment, and the type of investment. You have to owe tax, even when your fund is not sold and given you no returns.

Where these taxes come from:

1. When you own a fund:

   A mutual fund gathers cash from many investors and buys stocks, bonds, and other assets with a professional managing purchasing. An investor owns the mutual fund and also pays operational fees. Shares can increase or decrease in price, which will depend on how their companies are performing.

   When you own a fund, two things could incur taxes

   - The fund might give you dividends or interest from the assets.

- The professional might sell assets on a profit and give you a piece of that profit.

IRS Publication 550 can be used to see all the details about tax rules concerning investing.

Dividends/Interest Tax

- Dividends can be claimed by you or distributed and invested into a mutual fund. Even if it is automatically reinvested, you will still owe taxes on those dividends.
- Some bonds, such as Municipal bonds and Treasury, are tax-free, but generally, the income you will review from interest payments is taxable. So even if you reinvest the money quickly, you still owe taxes on them.
- A copy of money generated by dividends and returns will be given to the IRS, so you have to report them on your tax return. A form needs to be filled in called 1099-DIV for this purpose.

2. When you get capital gains

   Capital gains are distributed to investors annually.

- These are taxable; even if you reinvest in them, you still owe taxes on them.
- You have to report them in your tax return as well because the IRS will get a report of it.
- The tax will increase or decrease depending on the duration you held that fund. If you own it for more than a year, then the tax will be lowered.

3. When you sell your fund

If you sell your fund for more than you paid for, it will count as a capital gain, and you have to pay taxes for it. Most likely, you might have purchased all your funds slowly over time, so you have funds of different prices. You can get an investment tracker from the firm that will help you keep a record of all the gains and losses you have incurred.

It can be difficult to assess how much actual profit you make. However, you can judge individual shares and know what you are selling, then sell the oldest shares first. You can also use the average cost of all the shares. More details will be discussed in the later chapters.

Is One Stock Taxed Twice?

When you buy a mutual fund, you have to pay an annual tax on its earnings and also a capital gains tax at the time of sale. That might seem unfair, but it is not being taxed twice. By law, you have to pay tax for the gains you have accumulated relating to that stock, not the stock itself. Later, you are taxed because you have gotten a profit by selling the stock at a higher price.

Tips To Decrease Taxes

- Plan for the long term. You have to pay a higher capital gains tax if you sell your fund within a year.
- Use the money saved in IRA or Roth IRA to purchase mutual funds. These accounts grow wealth tax-free until money is withdrawn. You will not pay tax on withdrawals if you start using the money after 60 years of age and have the account for more than 5 years.
- Use 401k accounts to purchase shares. Money here is tax-deferred, and you only pay taxes after withdrawal.
- Know what kind of returns the funds give. Be sure not to fill your portfolio with lots of dividend-paying assets and lots of capital gain-giving assets. As we have discussed, they will lead to high taxes being charged. Index funds are a good choice

because buying and selling are not as often in these funds.

- Tax-loss harvesting is the selling of assets at a loss to discourage capital gains. Because of it, you will only pay taxes on net profit, which will be the amount you have gained, subtracted by the amount you have lost. This reduces the tax bill. You can sell your underperforming funds to do this.

- Get a tax professional to advise you on how to minimize taxes in every area of investing.

Penalties And Mutual Funds

Putting shares in 401k and other retirement accounts may help you with minimizing taxes, but they are subjected to penalties on early withdrawals. The penalty also depends on the reason for withdrawal.

Normally, the penalty fee ranges from 10-25% when taking money out of an IRA account prematurely.

How Do Penalties Work?

You can keep adding money on your retirement accounts, tax-free, and your wealth within the account also will grow tax-free. After the specified time of when you age 60 years, you have to pay income tax on withdrawals. If you take money out before you turn 60 and sell your shares, then by federal tax law, you are making an early withdrawal. You have to pay 10% on that withdrawal. Also, if you sell your shares in a traditional IRA account that you opened in under 2 years, then the penalty can go up to 25%.

Circumstances where penalties are waivered:

- If you are withdrawing to reimburse medical costs that exceed 7.5 % of your general gross income or 10% if you are under 65.
- If you want to cover certain education costs, for example, college tuition, the administrative fee charged by the school, books, equipment and supplies, board room costs, etc.
- If you want to buy a house
- If you withdraw the fund after becoming disabled

After-Tax Funds

If you purchase a share from a Roth IRA account, then you buy it with an after-tax fund. Many companies and employers give provisions for after-tax Roth contributions.

An after-tax contribution to your simple IRA account is also possible. You can buy shares from your principal amount and sell them without penalties, but you owe taxes on your fund's earnings.

No penalties are charged when you are out the principal money or the actual deposited amount of money from the account. However, if it has not been more than 5 years since you opened the account, then a 10% penalty and income tax are applied.

Reinvestment Charges

When reinvesting, the charges vary frequently and it becomes difficult to keep track of changes. The interest you earned from one asset can be taken out and given to separate security. You will learn more about this in chapter 8.

Early Redemption Fees

Some funds have the policy to put these fees so that you, the investor, get discouraged from selling the fund early on or prematurely. Short-term trading is harmful to the firm company as they are in the business for the long run; that is why these charges are imposed. The fees are limited to 2% by the SEC (Security and Exchange Commission). The fees are waived after a specific time, which ranges from one month to one year. We have discussed that funds with back-end load impose fees when those funds are sold prematurely, which is payable to the broker. Early redemption fees are a separate entity that is paid not to the broker but to the fund itself.

Exchange Fees

Mutual funds also carry with them exchange fees. These charges are applied when an investor exchanges a fund in their portfolio for another fund in the same fund family. This exchange is a type of sale that can bring in profit for the investor; hence these exchange events are taxable. In addition, any capital gains on these sales of shares need to be written down on your tax as well.

What To Do If You Cannot Pay Minimums?

The best thing to do is size up your investing wealth over time so that the returns are also high and more insignificant. However, there are other options. One thing you can do is use an online brokerage that can make your own stocks and ETF trades with only $5 charges.

You can also open an account in Robo advisors. Instead of an actual person, an online application will assist you in your investment management. You can set your investment goals and then let the application run without any supervision. There is no minimum for them, and if there is, it is very low. Some examples are:

- Betterment with a minimum $0
- Wealthsimple with a minimum $0
- Hedgeable with a minimum $1

Some Robo-advisors can be costly, so watch out for them; for instance, Vanguard Personal Advisor Service is $50,000.

Steps To Decrease Fees

Some funds have more expense ratios than others, so you need to look around before buying a fund. Passively managed funds and passive managers charge fewer fees than actively managed funds.

Passive managers copy the stock index and try to follow the market. Index fund and index ETF managers trade so that they are reaching the benchmark. Trades incur trading costs, but they are minimal.

Active managers choose funds meticulously, which incurs researching costs and generally have more transaction costs because they trade at a higher level. You will see all these expenses as MER.

It is questionable to say which one performs better, but it is better to cut as many costs as you can. You could get a better return on a passively managed fund than an actively managed one because there is less deduction.

Fact: Expense ratios are going down for both actively and passively managed funds. It was 0.68 and 0.14 during 2018 and became 0.66 and 0.13 respectively.

Investors have an eye for low-cost funds, and that is why many fund companies are giving less expensive options to choose from. This can also be shown by the popularity of Robo-advisors and companies building software for investors to build portfolios at a cheap price.

The cost of ETFs is better than other mutual funds. These fees are generally lower than what you pay for in mutual funds. However, mutual fund companies are lowering their costs to get more investors interested. Over the last two decades, ETF and mutual funds have lowered their price by half. Each company or fund is trying to increase the number of people buying their products. The funds are, therefore, giving competitive prices.

For mutual funds, the expense ratio is written in the fund's prospectus, but several other fees factor in as well. There are but not limited to:

- Management fees: This includes the salaries of the fund company's workers and advisor costs
- 12b-1 fee: These should be less than 1% of your returns. It includes bonuses of the fund company's workers and marketing expenses. It is an operational expense and, therefore, contained within the expense ratio.
- Account fee: These are only for investors that have accounts below a specific level.
- Others: These include custodial, legal, accounting, administrative expenses, and more. Moreover, the type of fund and policies of the investment firm also dictates changes in the amount.

All these fees are cut yearly, and based on the number of transactions (frequency), the charges of one transaction, and transferring of funds, more fee cost is added.

To buy the shares, you have to pay a load fee. This is about 5% of the amount being invested and is paid to the broker, the person selling the shares. These load fees can be avoided by purchasing no-load funds which are abundantly available directly from the fund companies.

ETFs fund management is not seen in the fund's statements, and they are deducted daily instead of annual from the NAV.

- They have lower fees than mutual funds. These are mostly passively managed and always "no-load."

You can even be charged $0 for some ETF trades, and normally it costs $10.

- The 12b-1 fee is not charged. These are marketing and distribution costs that the investor gives to the company to get more shareholders.
- Market-based trading is done. ETFs can be purchased and sold like stocks and bonds in marketing hours, so the sale does not affect the ETF.

When mutual funds are sold by their shareholders, they first redeem them from the fund. That means the fund must sell some assets for redemption. A capital gain distribution is seen when a fund sells an asset, and all its shareholders get it. The shareholders will pay income taxes on this capital gain also at the expense of transactions. ETF has no reason to liquidate, hence fewer expenses.

- Investors can use in-kind creation and redemption. You, as an investor, can sell stock shares for an equivalent portfolio that has the same number of ETFs. You can also exchange ETFs for a basket of stocks as well. This reduces paperwork and operational costs.

When you sell funds, lots of fees apply, which eats away your returns. Suppose you do not want to be disheartened at those cuts. In that case, you have to keep yourself informed about all the charges by reading each fund's prospectus carefully. Only by being mindful about these charges and making informed decisions can you turn over a significant profit. Remember that a little research can potentially save hundreds of your dollars in the future. Time is money and do you want to spend the time doing it yourself or do you want to spend the money to have someone do it for you? The next chapter will discuss both sides.

It is also important that you keep all the records of mutual fund purchases, gains, and charges, including reinvested returns.

Chapter 6 – Do I Buy Alone or Do I Pay the Piper?

You should look for ways to cut out fees, and buying a no-load fund is a way to do that. But it is for you to decide whether you want an investment broker to help you allocate your investments or not. For some people, it might be beneficial to get their advice and services during mutual investing.

To make a conscientious decision that will affect your future savings, you should know everything about them first.

Investment Brokers

If you are a beginner in mutual investing or investing in general, then a professional investment broker can help you break the ice and connect you with the market. They can have a lot of history of working with people in the investment industry and act as an in-between for the sellers and investors. They can help you find the best offers and put them in front of you. In addition, they help you buy assets like bonds and other securities from the market.

An investment broker can be a single person or multiple people under an institution or organization. They take the responsibility from the investors of trading and do multiple transactions on the investor's behalf. A single investment broker can be independent or working for a big brokerage firm like Morgan Stanley. You have to work with this individual to trade investments. This is also called a "regular broker." They are other types of brokers as well.

Another type of investment broker is a broker reseller. These people act as a third party connecting a small investor to a bigger broker.

Many brokers can be found that offer various services, and they can be categorized according to the service they provide. For example, suppose a broker can advise you on personalized investment and retirement plans. In that case, that person is known as a full-service broker.

Some brokers only offer the service of managing trades and not giving advice which is called discount brokers. If you are getting a broker off the internet, most likely, a broker is offering only the minimal service of purchasing and selling assets. Often, a firm acts as a broker for an investor, which is their client. In addition, the firm serves as a transaction agent for them.

Types Of Investment Brokers

You will need a broker to purchase and sell investments. This is the main purpose of a broker. They are licensed professionals that trade securities in the security exchanges. They can do a lot for you, but the services offered are different for every broker and brokerage firm. How many services you want and need will guide you to the kind of broker you want.

Full-Service Brokers

Most commonly, they are related to brokerage firms and work as their agents. They will assist you in many areas. They will arrange meetings to know your financial goals, show the results of their research and help you choose the best kinds of assets for your goals. They will be ahead of market news and discuss current trends, tax laws, and stock performance with you. These brokers can help individuals with a hefty investment portfolio and those who are looking for an expert to manage them. You need to be careful and look for people that have your best interest at priority. A person working for commissions or a third party will have different priorities and can sabotage your earnings in the future. That is why you need to look for an investment broker who has a fiduciary duty.

Fact: Fiduciary duty is a commitment by a person or a company to work according to the likes of another entity, a client, or a beneficiary. It is a duty undertaken to show loyalty and care.

Discount Brokers

These types of brokers take care of the buying and selling process of assets. You must be the one to specify the order, and they do not give their opinions or advice. They do not comment on your portfolio or give you a review. E-Trade and Ally are companies that operate online and offer to open brokerage accounts. These companies only provide services as discount brokers.

Investment Broker Fees

The fee is related to how many services they are offering you. Therefore, it depends upon how many purchases and trades you are conducting. They usually charge per transaction.

A discount broker will charge a lower amount because they are only providing minimal service. However, they will charge somewhere between $5-30 for each transaction.

On the contrary, a full-service broker will conduct thorough research and give expert opinions on every action relating to the investment. Their costs are significantly higher, with prices ranging up from $100 to $200 for each transaction. There is also an annual maintenance fee that we discussed in the previous chapter.

You need to remember that to open an account with a brokerage firm, you need to have a minimum amount of around $500 or maybe more. So be informed about all charges before you open an account with one.

Finding An Investment Broker

There is an abundance of brokers and brokerage firms that advertise heavily for your attention. It will be confusing to find one that you want, but there will bound to be one that checks all your boxes with so many choices.

First and foremost, you need to understand your financial goals and determine whether that investment broker has experience managing investment according to those goals. For example, if you think you are going to make a lot of trades, then prioritize lower fees. If you want to invest in a particular asset, make sure the broker has experience dealing with that asset.

Next, look at the price of that broker. It should be lower or equal to your budget. Do not overspend because the fee can build up over time and eat away your returns.

Figure out what kind of broker you want. Do you feel like you need some expert to help you along the way, or do you feel confident in your research and analysis skills?

List out all the brokers and brokerage firms that can be good candidates, and then compare them to each other. Some brokers offer online and mobile services that can be a plus. Maybe a broker with a lower minimum amount will be helpful to you.

Do your research of your chosen broker yourself. They must be a registered individual with the Financial Industry Regulatory Authority (FINRA).

Having or not having an investment broker is your decision, but you have to give it a serious thought to begin investing. If you are a complete novice and have very little confidence in the industry, then you might hire a full-service broker at the start. By discussing and talking with the individual or individuals or a firm, you will get a much better grip on handling assets on your own. Then, you can save money by getting discount brokers or no brokers in the future.

How To Avoid Fraud?

Every mutual fund has to file a prospectus and updates on shareholder's reports with the SEC. You have to read these prospectuses before investing in a mutual fund. You might be buying and managing your funds through advisors or professionals. Make sure they are registered with the SEC as well.

Is it worth it?!

An investment being successful could depend on you choosing a great investment broker. With a broad and changing industry like mutual funds, there are hundreds of opportunities available. You will get confused about what you want and what kind of investment suits you the most. Although, there is no concrete explanation for having a brokerage account through a broker.

To want average earnings and allow other professionals to get a piece of the profits is ok for you; you do not always need to set up a brokerage account. But, if you want to invest for a lot higher returns and want to stay investing for a long time with the mindset of staying ahead, you should consider joining in a partnership with a great investment broker.

Can A Stockbroker Help?

Setting up a brokerage account with an investment broker is a very different process than opening an account and hiring a manager to take care of investments. However, an investment broker can be a good decision to make life-changing wealth. It is because you will be the one in charge of your investment portfolio.

When you invest your money, there is always some professional pulling the strings of your money. They could be bank employees, fund managers, or investment professionals. A good broker will act as your knowledgeable assistant and guide you through the process of making great wealth. They will give you tools, advice, be on top of trends and help you determine what your long-term goals are. They will aid in the decision, not make it for you.

When Do I Need One?

There are many scenarios in which having a broker will be beneficial, and opening an investment account is a wise choice.

You can purchase and give away any stock that is accessible to your broker. If you have chosen a good broker, you can work in various markets and every company listed with them, like the New York Stock Exchange.

Foreign stocks are easily available to you as well. You will have more options available and choose the best stocks after assessing risks and benefits.

Many brokers do not just offer stock trading and mutual fund trading, but also other sorts of investments and other bank account products. As a result, you can have a wide variety of assets to choose from. A broker can give access to almost unlimited shops of investments. You will not need to open multiple accounts in multiple investment companies to purchase different assets.

Brokers conduct a lot of research, and you might find great details of funds and stocks before investing in them. The information can help you make a mindful judgment and help you recognize a compelling stock or fund.

Because many brokers are available, people and firms try to distinguish themselves by giving a broader service than advising on investing. For example, they can help you make a budgeting plan, provide mortgage calculators and give real estate research.

What makes an ideal investment broker is that they offer many services at a low price with a past performance showing promise in them. The fees should be low because there will be fund exchange commissions and account expenses as well. A good broker will provide you with multiple account facilities, the ability to open up different financial accounts, research, and advice regularly. They should offer you tax-favored accounts, like IRA retirement accounts and a normal brokerage account. A broker who understands your goals and takes time to discuss your financial objectives is an important aspect to search for when hunting for a broker.

We have talked about different types of assets, but the most valuable asset you have is time. If you are an indecisive person who chooses after long consideration or your research process takes a lot of time, you are wasting months. You will delay opening accounts, buying funds and stocks, be late, and doubt your strategy, which will cause you anxiety. Investment is a long game in which you gain interest returns over the years, building a substantial pillar of wealth from very little gains each month. If you get an ideal financial broker, you will not waste any of your priceless time and be confident in making decisions.

Most Popular and Dependable Brokerage Firms

Different companies offer different services, and you can choose them based on your goals and objectives.

TD Ameritrade

For beginners, this is the place to start. It provides you with great investment knowledge and helpful experience. They offer free stocks and ETF, no minimums, free learning through websites and phone apps.

The downside is that they pay very low returns, which are around 0.05%. You can make more if you want by moving money into money market funds.

E-Trade

As the name indicates, the company specializes in making trades easier between investors. It offers no minimums, no commission fee for stock exchange and ETF trades. There is a contract fee of 0.5-0.65% for option trades. A standard website is user-friendly and not overwhelming to a beginning investor. It offers many services like screening tools, portfolio analysis, and education through apps as well. The apps are extremely well designed and detailed. Suppose you want to quickly start trading with the little money you have lying around. In that case, the company offers prebuilt portfolios you can purchase to enter the market directly.

The downside is that foreign markets and foreign currencies do not get represented on the site. In addition, you cannot import account details from other financial institutions and external accounts either, so you will not get a clear picture of your net worth.

Merrill Edge

They offer the best customer service on the market. It offers no minimums, no commission per stock trade. For beginners, the website has an abundance of resources that you can explore. The apps have features that make it easy for you to see how well your portfolio is doing and what is affecting it. There is an online chat option available along with 24/7 technical and trading assistance. If you have $100,000 saved up, you qualify for even more benefits and make more money.

The downside is that per its contract, the options trading fee and interest rate are a little high. You cannot participate in the trade of cryptocurrency, futures, and futures options either.

Making Online Purchases of Mutual Funds

A long time ago, people could only invest via a broker, money manager, or some other finance professional. But now, with a handheld phone or a laptop, you can purchase mutual funds anywhere you want. If you have a retirement account, the financial institution where you opened it can buy mutual funds for you, but you can only trade a few times using them in a limited market.

Now, where to buy it? There are hundreds of websites offering trades, but there are three places you have to look first to buy mutual funds

Investment Companies

You can directly purchase the fund of your choice through investment companies. They are the ones managing and offering them. These are publicly traded, e.g., T.Rowe Price, or privately traded, e.g., American Century. A firm has different funds to appeal to a myriad of customers. By buying directly, you will not pay commissions or brokerage fees. But, you are limited to the company's funds only.

Investment-Cum-Financial Service Companies

The restriction of being limited to one fund company is overcome through these companies. You are allowed to trade by using an in-house account, mutual funds, and ETFs from other firms. The two big companies are Vanguard Group and Fidelity Investments. However, if you buy another firm's fund, there are extra costs and commissions.

Brokerages

You can open an online brokerage account, but it will be the most expensive option. You will be charged fees for commissions, setup, and maintenance. However, you will be free to choose any kind of mutual fund. If you look around, you can find low-cost ones very easily. Some of them are E-Trade and Betterment. The big giants, like Charles Schwab, have also launched their digital platforms and online trading options.

Setting Up an Account

You will first log on to the website and click the option that says "Open account" or "Let's get started". You will give your basic information, choose an account type. You will need to specify whether you want dividends automatically reinvested or saved up. If everything is in order, your account will be ready within a week.

Purchasing Funds

Every site has its unique designs, but all of them will show a ticker in front of a fund. You have to click the ticker and specify the amount you want to invest in it, determining how many shares of the fund you can buy. Mutual funds are different from stocks this way because you can only buy a stock at a fixed price.

After filling the trade request, at the end of the day, the price of the fund is calculated. After that, you will know how many shares you have purchased. The purchase will be confirmed within two business days.

Non-Publicly Offered Mutual Funds

As the name indicates, these funds are not offered to the public because of their high risk and high returns, and only the wealthy can access them. These are not registered as securities but private placement. You have to be an accredited investor to purchase them

Fact: An accredited investor is a person that meets a specific income and net worth value, and they are allowed to invest in non-registered funds.

These funds are aggressively managed, and various plans are applied so that they give a good return or an "alpha" to the investor. Thus, they are also referred to as hedge funds.

Drawbacks

There are three main disadvantages of these funds:

1. Lack of liquidity: Because of limited investors, it will be difficult to quickly sell the fund.
2. High fees: More aggressive management means more charges and also more tax cuts along with gains.
3. Low disclosure: Because they are less regulated, investors have very little clue of what manages the fund.

Self-Investing

You have to be certain about your financial goals and long-term plans before self-investing. You will spend a lot of time researching because you are the only one responsible for buying a good fund.

You can self-invest through

- Online investing

  You can purchase and sell assets with a click of a mouse. This is possible through many cost-efficient brokerage firms. Doing trading and investing from these firms is known as online investing.

- Direct investing

  This is also known as FDI (foreign direct investment). This involves investing in an out-of-country institute or business that will collect interest in the said enterprise. You can gain interest earnings without the traditional way of buying stocks and shares.

- Dividends Reinvesting

  In this type of program, you can allow the firm to use your earned dividends, to buy shares and stocks.

Should you self-invest and manage funds? You may have been looking around at stock data and thinking about doing some management yourself. That is when you have to answer some questions which will make it clear to you whether you are cut out for self-investing or not.

Do you know the fundamentals of business? Many people do not know where most of a company's profit comes from. Thus, they will not be able to judge the profits if a change occurs and will not be ahead of trends. For example, you may think coca-cola makes its money by selling bottles of soda. That is not the case. They make the most money by selling their concentrated syrups to bottlers who make sodas and sell them to retailers. If there was a policy change that affected the bottler's work, you would have no idea why your big company stock did not do so well.

Are you as well informed about investing as you think you are? If you are thinking about managing investment by yourself, quickly take a clean page and write the investment strategy and principles your current portfolio is following, and features of your stock bought, and why you bought them.

If this seems like a hard task, it might not be the right time for you to think about self-management. This exercise shows that you do not follow the progress of your stocks and have become detached from them. Detachedness is not always a bad thing. It can help you make decisions without emotions hindering your business mindset.

If you complete this task within seconds, then you have the knack for self-managing investments. You should know what kind of principles you follow, like someone having a

Graham and Dodd School of value investing principles, will look for a low price to earnings, low price to book values, and stable dividends in stocks and funds.

Do you understand cash flows? If you cannot set a discount annuity stream, it is not a good idea to manage your investment. Discount annuity stream determines the present value of the annuity which directly affects how much interest-based earnings you will receive. Terms and aspects of investment are broad and many factors affect the funds. You need to have the ability to calculate the valuation of funds and assets independently. Otherwise, you will find yourself lost with untruthful sellers that will sell you seemingly attractive but costly investments. Untruthful sellers will not have your best interest and take your money without discussing future charges and leave your wallet bleeding. They might lie or hide important information. Protect yourself and be aware of them.

Can you stop yourself from aggressive accounting? Aggressive accounting is the practice of overstating a business's performance, financial or otherwise. In a company's yearly report, the net income and earnings from shares are not 100% accurate. They are rough estimates, and there will be estimates in the cleanest balance sheets you come across. These may be the number of customers that will not pay their bills, future returns on pension assets, level of products returned, etc.

Fact: A balance sheet is a financial statement that a company releases showing its assets, liabilities, and shareholder equities.

If you start aggressively using these numbers, they can show better numbers than they give. You need to protect yourself by identifying and not engaging in them. If you cannot indicate when a company uses aggressive accounting, it is better not to start self-investing.

Do you know correlation risks? What do you consider more diverse? For example, "Portfolio X" has 10 stocks made up of 3 banks, 5 real estate investment trusts, and 2 insurance companies. Or "Portfolio Y," which has 5 assets consisting of one real estate investment trust, one giant company, one oil company, and one international mutual fund.

If your answer is "Portfolio X," then self-investing can wait. You are more diverse when buying five unrelated stocks than twice as many stocks in the same industry. That is because, during bad times, the entire sector is affected and not just one or two areas, for instance, the real estate collapse of the 1980s.

In finance and business, the degree to which one factor affects two different securities and causes them to shift is known as correlation. If the effect is similar and more in sync then it is said that there is correlation risk. When you have funds that move in the same way, they undermine diversity in your portfolio. You have to have securities that move independently from each other as much as possible.

Are you emotional? Many investors get scared at the thought of buying stocks when they are at a low price. Whenever there is a sale of food or clothing, we hurriedly buy them and snatch the opportunity. This is not the case with investing. People want to wait for the prices to start rising to become confident of a purchase. This is a bad habit. Even though rising prices ensure that the fund is going to do good in the future, it is not a guarantee and you will purchase the fund at a higher cost, causing you to lose profit.

If you can handle your stock's value going down by 50% without panicking, then you can think about managing your investment. Of course, hiring a professional will cost higher than self-investing, but self-investing requires time and mental strength. If you think you have the capabilities to achieve self-management, then, by all means, go for it.

Only after you are able to answer the questions above will you be advised to continue with self-investing; otherwise, there is no hesitation in getting some help as a beginner. Being humble and admitting your lack of knowledge is the first step towards achieving great experiences. Once you have decided whether you want to get a broker or not, you can start trading with funds. You have to know how to manage them during the course of your investing period.

Chapter 7 – How Often Do I Check on My Money?

You need to purchase funds after carefully understanding each of them and being fully aware of their purpose. Let us suppose you have bought many funds and ETFs. Now, you just have to wait and let your mutual funds grow wealth over time. After a person has invested a lot of money, they are overrun with anxiety and develop a habit of compulsively checking the status of their accounts and the number of funds they have. Some people might be a bit more reasonable and check once a month, but there can be some who have had fear taken over them and check every hour or so.

We check our status during investing because:

- To assess whether the strategy is working and the funds are behaving in the way we want them to.
- Depending on the current news or trend of that time, people keep looking at new opportunities or threats that might affect their investments. Suppose a person thinks that a threat can be avoided or an opportunity cannot be missed. In that case, that person will review their portfolio and act accordingly.
- People check the status of mutual funds more often than other types of investment because it is easier. In

addition, our devices have made them accessible anywhere.

Frequency For Looking at My Investments

There are many good reasons for looking at the status of the funds but do we have to every hour, week, and month. We need to keep checking but not at an unhealthy frequency.

Before investing, you might have taken a comprehensive look at your goals and financial objectives. You should have based your decisions, keeping certain factors in mind. These may include expected return value, profile risks you are willing to take, for how long you will be investing, what asset type and asset class you want to pick, the age at which you will sell all your funds, etc.

Many people often invest in the advice of friends and family that they think have more experience and knowledge. Many people hire a professional instead to work their mutual funds for them. It is unfortunate that these people do not take the time to learn about investing themselves. Instead, people assume it is not for them or think that they are not smart enough but act on complex decisions every day. For example, when you decide to get insurance for your vehicle, you look at each factor and feature very thoroughly and research endlessly to get the best offer. The same is with buying a house and investing in real estate.

Others need to understand that to invest in mutual funds successfully, you need a bit of understanding of their work. You do not need to be a professional; you do not need to get a degree in finance. Just keep finding basic knowledge about the subject and growing your mind. When a person has gone through the phase of making a portfolio, trading assets and applying different strategies, and taking risks, they understand what is the best frequency for checking your wealth in investments.

After you have invested and bought all of your funds with the initial amount, then you should check your portfolio every 6 months or twice a year. Do not check your investments too much because it can lead you to make bad decisions. Emotions, greed and fear take over our rational choices and turn them into irrational decisions.

For example, you have put money in equity funds to buy a car in the next 10 years. Equity funds are not stable and keep fluctuating in price constantly. If you have a habit of checking your portfolio's worth daily, hourly, or even weekly, then you will be overrun with emotions. You can only make a lot of wealth in investing by waiting out a long period. If you have a goal and have invested for 10 years, you have no reason to keep checking the amount and values daily. Imagine the funds being down 20% one day. You will have a compulsion to sell those funds. Now, imagine the fund's value increasing by 30%. You will think to yourself that this is a good time to buy more investments. Greed and fear will take over you, and you will suffer losses.

These emotions cannot be avoided, as they are normal human traits. Being successful in investing depends upon you not basing your decisions on the behavior of the funds and on the advice from people that have no care about your money and investments, but on your own experience and knowledge.

If you wait out long enough, the best performing funds and average performing funds almost give the same amount in return. There is not a significant difference. Even if you let your funds work in the background and follow the market, they will do well and give you a profit.

Factors To Keep in Mind When Checking Your Investments

After passing 6 months, you will check your funds for a deep review and rebalancing of the portfolio. There are a few aspects to keep in mind when doing it:

- Any change in the fund manager. If, after a certain time, a fund's manager has been replaced, you should research and assess the new manager. Talk with your financial advisor about his or her effect on your current portfolio. Every manager has their strategies and mindset, so there can be a significant difference in the fund's performance. If you think there is a change in fund manager, just call your broker or brokerage firm and they will confirm it for you.

- Your fund has gone through a scheme merger. The company of a fund sometimes reallocates their existing fund, which means that an average manager manages the same amount of capital but in fewer assets, fewer classes, and investment styles. Imagine if you have invested a significant portion in large-cap equity, which is scheme A. After some time, that same company has merged into scheme B and made the fund multi-cap or short cap. Your initial objective is lost. You have to sell that fund and purchase a new fund that fulfills your plans.
- Some funds are going through closure. Sometimes a fund can close down due to various reasons that you cannot control. In such cases, the company closes and returns the money to its shareholders. The mutual fund contacts their investors and informs them of this situation. Later on, you have to make changes to your portfolio.
- Investing is a risk, and most of the time, funds follow the market highs and lows. However, after 6 months of having a fund, you can see its performance during this duration. If the fund does not act according to your strategy and has been

incurring losses, then you need to evaluate the situation, your current financial goals and take the necessary course of action. For example, you may have to sell the fund.

Frequent checking of your fund status can be harmful to your mind and finances. Instead, take a glance at them once or twice a year, and take action only when needed and after analyzing the situation. You can review your portfolio when a life-changing event happens, such as marriage, the birth of a child, a death in the family, etc.

Who Can Check Investments More Frequently?

The performance of your portfolio is your future wealth and wellbeing, so you need to address this question carefully. Of course, you can check your portfolio more often, but only if you are an active investor. An active investor will be continuously purchasing and selling stocks and funds. Needless to say, that they have to monitor them more often and sometimes daily.

Someone investing in themselves and not relying on a professional will also need to be ahead of trends. But, the most important task and time-consuming work will be research. They need to research different types of funds and stocks available so that they can buy one at the best price, with the best perks.

People investing in short-term and ultra short-term funds can also check their accounts and portfolio more frequently. However, their respective brokers will manage any hindrance their portfolio may face, so there is not much to worry about. Opening the portfolio once a month may be enough.

If you have followed the instructions written in this book, you will have a well-diversified and properly managed portfolio. Most people usually pick long-term funds and assets that grow substantial wealth to ensure their comfy retirement. People that have diversified, managed, more long-term investments do not need to check their portfolios often. Once or twice a year is enough.

If you are a young investor that is saving up for a distant future or retirement, then checking once in six months is a good frequency.

Checking and monitoring your money is your own choice. However, many long-term investors also review their portfolios every three months, and some argue that once per month is most preferred. It largely depends on what type of fund you have, how long you are investing for, your goals, and whether you are doing it yourself or hiring a professional.

If the type of fund undergoes massive fluctuations like equity funds, which do not affect future performance, there is no need to check your funds and trends. If you are investing for a long period, then fluctuations in the present

134

will stabilize and not affect your returns. If your goals are to buy that house 10 years later, then there is no reason to check the money in your brokerage account every few months either. By hiring a professional, a broker, or a brokerage account, you cut out all the management work and forget about the fact that you even invested any money.

Anxiety and Investments

There is no need to become anxious. In investing, the most vulnerable person who gets the most worried and develops problematic behavior are long-term investors. When they start to look at the fund's value every week or every day, they get anxious. Anxiety can be tiring to the mind and cause harm to you in the long run.

Anxiety is a normal reaction to stressful situations. It puts you into a fight or flight response, and your body gets ready for action. If you have invested long-term and have a habit of micro-checking, you will become anxious more often, and your body will start to show symptoms. You can develop, in severe cases, increased heart rate, palpitations, and chest pain. You are at risk of hypertension and heart disease. Your health, physical and mental, should be treated as your most important asset.

When you check daily the fund's progress, you will see the value become high one day and low the next. However, that does not mean your fund is doing well or bad. Short-term fluctuations are a norm in the financial market, and almost every fund witnesses it. If you see average market fluctuations, there are many short-term falls even though it has been increasing steadily throughout the decade. Once you see a decrease in value, which is not uncommon, you will become anxious every time.

Emotional Investing

If you develop an unhealthy habit and get extremely anxious, then your decisions might be clouded by emotions, and you can potentially hurt your portfolio. Being anxious will not only ruin your body but also your future investments.

The objective is to buy when the prices are low and sell when the prices are high.

After seeing your fund's value plummet a little, you might start to get ideas about selling the fund early at a lower cost. On the other hand, by seeing your fund increase in value, you will be enticed to buy more of that fund when prices are high because you think they will do good in the future. Both actions will lead you to diverge from your objectives, and you will only incur losses with this behavior.

We are all humans, so if you think that you cannot handle your feelings and not emotionally invest, then it is better that you hire a broker and never look at the fund except when needed. Short-term performance is not indicative of long-term profit or return value.

Practice Self-discipline

You should make a comfortable schedule for looking at the investment numbers. Set a reminder or ask your advisor to contact you when the time comes. After setting a reminder, you should forget about your investment. Keep more distance between you and your portfolio viewing website or app. Delete the app and restrict access to that website if your temptations have a habit of controlling you.

The distance between you and the portfolio will help you make long-term, good financial decisions that will be rational and based on a good strategy. You will lose stress and become less anxious when investing as well. For a long-term investor, short-term fluctuations should be nothing more than irrelevant noise.

Developing self-discipline is key to creating a good investing experience. To develop self-discipline, you need to first acknowledge your behavior honestly. You have to first know you have a problem before you try to remove it. You need to remove all the items that trigger your temptations, such as seeing your investment firm's app on your screen. Now, develop an alternative plan to follow when you feel the need to check your funds. Distract yourself with other interests or go to a place with no internet access. Have your partner, family, or friend help you as well. They can call you out when you are stepping out of line. Many people think that they can avoid their habits, but they are ingrained into your body. Never think that you can follow through with self-discipline with only your willpower. You would not have a problem in the first place if your willpower was strong enough.

Long Term Investing – How to Go About It?

Many years ago, there was a study to determine what kind of investor receives the best returns or the best strategy to invest. Fidelity Investments, a big investment company, conducted this study in the United States to outperform their own and investor's returns. It was found out in that study that people who got the highest returns and grew their wealth the most were people that had completely forgotten about their assets for years and even decades. Many people who had the highest returns were later found to be deceased for a long time. It was concluded by this study that the most profitable strategy, which is also the most beneficial to the investor and investor portfolio, is to turn a complete blind eye to the investments and let them run smoothly in the background. The best strategy is to do nothing.

Similar stories arise in different parts of the world as well, further solidifying the truth. One day, you could have bought 30,000 shares when you were young and earning way more than your expenditure. Later on, you get married, buy a house and start to have children. The investment you bought will turn from an exciting adventure to a faint memory over the years. After some 25 to 30 years, you might have a premonition to check upon those funds as a nostalgic reminder or general curiosity. You might find out that those shares you had bought so many years ago are now worth more than 100× times the amount they were back then. You would plan an early retirement in such a case.

The number of shares may be exaggerated in the above scenario. Still, if you only check your portfolio once every year, chances are that you can allocate more and more funds to it as time passes, giving you the same growth and profit in the future.

Long-term investments can lead to some great wealth building, but not many people don't have an idea of how long-term investments should be. Some people assume that it means an investment that grows for decades, and some assume that it is everything except day trading. With misconceptions and our friends and family advising without consequences, you are bound to get confused and may have wrong ideas of your own.

It depends on the asset or the type of security, bonds, or stocks. Long-term investment can be in your portfolio for at least a year and as long as 40 years or more. When professionals and experts discuss long-term investments and long-term growth, they often refer to a time of seven to ten years. There is no upper limit of years for long-term funds.

For tax purposes and calculation of liabilities, stocks and equity mutual funds are mostly held for more than one year and labeled as long-term investments. That is because one year is too little time for equity funds to show profits. Some other types of investment have a three years holding requirement to regard themselves as a long-term investment.

Why are some investments regarded as long-term? Some securities and assets, like equity funds, are unstable and fluctuate enormously by nature. The returns are very high, but there are extreme levels of crest and troughs. For example, in an overall 5 years period, an equity fund might grow 79%. But in one of those years, the fund could have dropped about 10%, or there could be two consecutive years that this fund does poorly. If you only had invested for one year or less, you could have incurred great losses and missed out on an opportunity of a lifetime. The accumulation of great years, plus some bad ones, make equity a high return giving a choice. This is the argument used when people acquire volatile investments, such as equity, talk about long-term investing.

Investment and different types of securities have their cycles, in which, in the end, they give a sharp rise and only increase to stay at that rate. For example, the cycle for equity lasts for 5 to 7 years and not 1 to 2 years. This is also true for long-term stocks. Before the cycle ends, the fund will go through a down phase and a stagnated phase in which it will neither rise nor fall significantly. To get a substantial profit, which only these kinds of funds provide due to their volatility, you need to keep investing until the end of the cycle, which means sticking to that fund and not selling it for seven years. This is done via a systematic investment plan which makes you follow through the entire cycle. If you do this, then an almost guaranteed huge return is ensured.

Motivation During Long-Term Investment

If you are still doubting your decisions and letting short-term rises and falls affect you, then here is another example to show you why long-term investments work. Value research conducted a study in 2017 to show how much profit and loss investors gather when investing for different periods. It was found that, on average, for the investment that followed a systematic investment plan or strategy, the loss of that investment is zero to minimal.

A typical fund running for three to four decades has an incredible amount of data to explore and analyze. Looking at one such fund, you see the average losses and profits the fund has gathered over one year period. In the study, the profit was more than 160%, and losses were around -57%. Now, we can see the average profit and losses the fund had gathered over two years. The profit was found to be 82%, and losses were at -34%. The same was done for three years. The profits were at 63%, and losses incurred were -18%. At five, profits were 54% and losses a mere 4%. This indicates that the loss becomes more and more negligible. The data used were all annualized figures.

You can see that you can gain a lot more than long-term investments in one year, but you can also lose a great amount as well. The risk you are willing to take should align with your investment goals, and if you are a beginner investor with little to no experience, it is advised to stay away from riskier options.

When you are interested in long-term investments, be sure to check the period lasts for, or more than, five years at least to get the best risk to profit ratio.

By following the advice above, you will be able to invest with ease and confidence. Your attitude towards investing should not be timid but curious. Every time you come across an acronym or a term you do not know, be eager to learn and ask about them. Most of your knowledge and intuition will come from experiencing the investment market yourself.

After making a portfolio and putting the funds of your choice into them, you will start earning some extra money and growing wealth. You will need to let it grow for some time before it can give a good return. Till that time arises, check on that fund when need is, talk to your advisor for further future endeavors you can explore, and try to put feelings away from investing as far as possible.

When you start seeing money grow in your accounts, you will be tempted to take it out or spend it. Fortunately, you can do a lot of things with that money that is discussed in the next chapter.

Chapter 8 – I Am Making Money in My Funds, Now What?

Waiting for a few years is crucial for seeing an increase in your account. However, once you have started to see some cash build-up, you might have certain impulses that may trigger you to waste this long-awaited gift of your patience.

Do not mindlessly spend the money you have gained through investing. To avoid making bad decisions, it is better to make plans ahead of time before seeing that you have gathered a good sum. Of course, the money and choice are yours, so you can do anything you want; however, there are certain options that you might want to keep in mind.

Reinvesting

This is the action of buying new shares in the company stock or unit using dividends and interest returns received from the same company's fund. Any sort of income distribution can be used to increase more investment opportunities in the same company.

By reinvesting, you can greatly grow the value of your unit, whether it be a stock, ETF, or any other mutual fund. With each year passing by, the number of shares will grow, and

144

so will the returns. As a result, you will get a greater return, and also, companies encourage this kind of process because you are buying more of their shares.

The amount that will be used for reinvesting will be gathered from previously received dividends and interest distribution received from the ownership of the original shares. These dividends and distributed amounts, if not reinvested, will be saved in the investor's account in the form of cash. When you choose reinvestment, most of the time, companies use that money to invest in their funds. If you do not reinvest, the dividend money is saved in your account and will stay the same amount forever.

DRIPS – Dividend Reinvestment Plans

The full form of DRIPS is Dividend reinvestment plans. The companies or firms can set up a program or system for you in which you can efficiently offer up your dividends and returns for reinvestment. The companies give investors an easy way to go about it through these plans.

Companies and corporations themselves provide these investment plans and other types of similar plans, for instance, master limited partnership or real estate investment trust. They are also a type of reinvestment plan. Although it is easy and encouraged to apply for this program, the fund company has the potential to stop you from reinvesting.

From a brokerage platform election, investors of publicly traded stocks can enter these DRIPS. The brokerage firm offers this plan when opening up your account, and you can ask your firm about it anytime in the future after not accepting it at first.

If the firm offers this plan, then the investor can shift their interests from the firm during this period. The fund does not need normal commission fees in reinvestment, and you can freely buy the new shares.

Income Generation

People that have a goal to generate income through investment are more inclined towards it. This is because every type of investment, including reinvestment, can add more returns and profits and thus more income to the investor. In addition, income investments are focused on generating a cycle of returns that could be treated as an income for the investor.

One prime example of a great income-generating fund is VHDYX or the vanguard high dividend yield fund. It gives one of the highest dividends in the market as of today. With this fund, you can reinvest all the dividends you will receive and get a huge sum of fractional shares. However, these programs can change, and without warning, so you have to keep that in mind.

The downside is that you have to be careful about taxes. Because taxes are still put on the dividends that you have reinvested, it does not matter that you have not taken it out of the account. For more detail, you can revisit chapter 5.

Fact: For a risk-free investment generation of income, you can buy some zero-coupon bonds, which is a bond whose face value gets repaid on the date of maturity. They issue no coupon payments and are fixed income generating instruments.

Downsides of Reinvestment

A huge sum is generated because of reinvestment, but that does not mean it is a perfect system. Sometimes the reinvestment rate becomes a hassle to handle. The reinvestment rate is when the amount of interest you get is taken out of one fixed income asset to another asset. Another way to explain it is that reinvestment rate is the investor's earnings, which comes when they buy a new bond while processing a callable bond called a due. This is because the interest rate is declining.

Fact: A callable bond is a bond that an investor can redeem before its maturity time comes.

An investor that is doing constant reinvesting might end up with reinvestment risk. This is because that investor cannot reinvest his cash flows at a similar rate of current investment return. This can happen with any type of asset.

Normally, the principal investing money is mostly invested on higher returning investment, and with reinvestment, that is not possible as you can only buy the same company's assets. This problem is not seen in fixed income security reinvestment, in which the amount given to you does not fluctuate due to interest rate and market changes. Therefore, you need to first assess your portfolio, whether you want to diversify, take a broader chunk of different types of assets, or rebalance funds.

For example – you can buy a Treasury note of $100,000 and is expected to grow to $6,000 in 10 years with a 6% interest rate. After 10 years, the interest rate drops to 4% and gives you only $4000 in earnings over the next 10 years. If the interest rate rises instead of falling, the company can sell the note before its maturity date, and you will lose some initial investing money.

Reinvesting Dividends

There are multiple benefits to reinvesting dividends instead of just taking that money out of your IRA or brokerage account. A dividend is paid by the company after the board of directors issues a declaration date. You will receive your dividend on this date, and it becomes your legal right after the date has been issued.

Dividends, sometimes, are reinvested directly into shares for you, and you buy more of the company's funds. The more shares you have of the company, the more dividends you will receive. A company has 4 million shares of common stock outstanding. They give a dividend of $0.5 for each share. So, the company pays 2 million dollars in dividends. If you own 100 dividends, you will get $50; subsequently, if you have 1000 shares, then you will get $500.

For example: Company dividend budget= 4000000*0.5 = $ 2 million

Each share receives = $ 0.5

Then, if you have 100 shares, you will receive = 100*0.5 = $50

If you have 1000 shares, you will receive = 1000*0.5 = $500

The benefits of dividend reinvestment can be very helpful to you because:

- They are cheap. You will not need to pay the normal commission fees to the brokerage firm and still get more shares.
- The process is automatic, easy to set up, and requires no oversight.
- Sometimes brokerage firms and brokers discourage you from buying fractional shares, but you can do that by reinvestment of dividends.
- You will increase your portfolio every time a dividend is received in your account.
- You will get a substantial growth in returns and your wealth through the compounding effect. Ultimately, you will buy more shares, which will give more returns, that can be used to buy more shares, and so on.

Who should not consider reinvestment? Unfortunately, despite the obvious advantages, there can be some aspects of your life that are not suited for this preposition.

When you are nearing the age of retirement. You have options to generate income through social security, RMDs, or required minimum distribution and also have access to pension annuities. These contain less risk than reinvestment, so be sure to view all your options before deciding on. When your assets are not doing so well.

Fluctuations in the market are common, and if the share sees a falling rate for two consecutive years, then do not consider reinvestment as a valid option. On the other hand, if your stock has not been producing dividends and you have reasons to believe it will continue to be unchanged, then it is better to sell the stock.

When do you want to diversify your portfolio?

Reinvestment increases the number of shares within the same company, so you do not have the chance to buy stocks and assets of your choice. You are afraid of out-balancing your portfolio. If a company is doing well for a long time, a big portion of your investments will belong to that company because it has continuously been increasing its number of shares. If one year a fall in prices occurs, you will face a great loss. That is why it is important to diversify your portfolio.

Growth Reinvestment Led To

Company XYZ has a moderate dividend rate of issuing $0.5 for each share. Imagine if the stock price increases annually 10% and the rate increases $0.05 each year. Now, you have bought shares using $20,000 when the stock price is $20, so you will end up with 1000 shares. In the first month, your dividend will be $500, using the math explained above.

Now, in the second year, the stock price is $22, and you buy extra shares using your dividend. So you will have 22.73 more shares.

Your dividend = $500

Share price = $22

Number of extra shares = 500/22 = $22.73

Total number of shares = 1000 + 22.73 = $1022.73

You can buy fractional shares with reinvestment so the $0.73 is no issue.

You will get a return of $0.55 in the second year and for $1022.73 shares. Thus, you will receive $562.50 (1022.73*0.55). The stock price is $24.2, so you buy an additional $23.24 (562.50/24.2) shares using your dividend amount. Now, you own 1045.97 shares which are worth $25,312.47.

On the upper end, Treasury funds give $6000 returns on a 10 years holding period, but you have just earned nearly $6,000 within two years. The amount will only substantially grow with time.

The important thing to note is that the company is continuing to progress and thrive. Therefore, your portfolio should be diversified, and you should reinvest in all areas. If you see a company struggling for a long time, then reinvest it somewhere else.

Withdrawal Plan

A withdrawal plan is just as its name would suggest, a plan for withdrawing cash from your financial investment account and mutual funds. This plan usually tells you at what times you have to take money out of the account. After reaching retirement, this plan is put into use to create an income stream, or a steady supply of money which will be deposited in your bank monthly, like an income.

How do withdrawal plans work? A withdrawal plan is referred to as a systematic withdrawal plan as well. This is because the investor will receive a portion of the returns on predetermined intervals and work as their payment structure. The plan can also encompass any liquidating strategy from the fund portfolio. For example, an investor can have a portfolio filled with equity funds. They could sell some of their equity funds annually to generate income for retirement or any other purpose.

The plan sets up a flow for the investor that gives them a consistent stream of money throughout their life. This can be set as a portion of trust of family corporation setup. In a family corporation set up, every child receives a smaller piece of the withdrawn money.

Benefits Of Having Withdrawal Plans

Using this strategy, you can keep getting money for a long time and still have money left in the account for further investment opportunities. Thus, the money will grow and keep giving returns through mutual funds.

You can make periodic withdrawals; the investors can get better and higher average sale prices for their return values. They can avail better asset prices that they will not have if they withdraw all the money at once. There is also the added benefit of tax advantages. If you are an experienced investor, you know that withdrawal plans are used as a strategy to reduce taxes pinned on their long-term gains. That is because the withdrawal money comes from the capital.

If the investment in your portfolio is doing well and rising consistently, then a systematic withdrawal plan can leave the investor with continuous income generation and letting the money grow simultaneously. Investors do not usually accumulate big amounts of money to stop their growth once they reach a phase in their life and start spending. Instead, they have a period called the accumulation phase, and after that, they put their withdrawal plan into action while continuing investing.

This is done through good management of portfolios, slowly and gradually selling some of their assets, and putting cash into income-generating securities. But, of course, a person can also buy an annuity or do so many other tasks that can help them go through their retirement with ease.

Disadvantages Of Having Withdrawal Plans

Suppose that it is a bad time to sell your assets at this particular time because they are falling in price. However, you have to sell those assets to maintain your withdrawal plan. Moreover, you have to sell more securities to reach your minimum income needs.

Taking Out Money from Mutual Funds for Day to Day Stuff

You can use this money for the goals you assigned for yourself, such as buying a house or paying for tuition. This is how you would cash out the money.

1. Call your broker

   Many firms have a toll-free number that you can contact freely. You might never need to call, as most transactions can happen online easily. You may have purchased your funds through accounts and firms where you can find the contact information on mails and emails.

2. Place order

   Select the number of shares you want to sell or set a dollar value. Then, input all the information requested or convey the information to a representative on a phone if you are calling to sell your shares. If you are directly contacting the company, you might need to fill a form, but it has become an unpopular method.

3. Delivery

   You have to tell your firm how you want to receive the returns of the sale. If an account is involved, such as brokerage, then you will receive the money in the account as cash. Then you will have to use an electronic bank transfer or write a paper check to receive the money.

4. Remember Taxes

If you sell a fund and reinvest it using an IRA account, you will not incur taxes. However, if you want an early withdrawal of the money, then the rules will apply that are written in IRS Publication 550.

5. Remember fees

Take into account that some funds carry back-end loads and that you have to pay them upon the sale of that fund.

What Happens When Selling Mutual Funds?

Redeeming mutual fund shares is a simple task. The funds cannot be traded between the market hours, and you can only sell the funds at the end of the day. The price or NAV is fixed at 4 P.M. EST. Like a lot of business redemptions, the process takes one or two business days. The fund companies have reserves so that they can pay redemption and not sell shares at inopportune times.

With mutual funds, you will be able to generate a regular stream of income through your retirement years. In addition, if you start to invest early in life, you will be able to quit your job quite early and never worry about mundane office work ever again.

To get that early retirement, you need to allocate a big chunk of your wealth, usually by saving up for investing and wait for one or two decades. The growth is slow, but on a large scale, you will be independent financially at the age of 40. If you are working to invest in your parents, spouse, and children, even more money can be invested. You might be able to retire by age 30 and go on vacations, travel, and do whatever you want.

The goal of investing is to establish an income generation stream or significant wealth that will support you throughout your life.

Conclusion

When you step into adulthood, you realize that school has not prepared you for the future. You do not know how to get a job, nor do you have any idea about taxes or renting/buying a home. You have to learn everything on the fly when you move out of your parent's house. Investment is just another one of these hurdles that you have to conquer through experience. There is much to learn, and it can be quite intimidating, considering it involves a lot of money, but there is nothing to be scared of.

You knew that you had to buy a house or a car someday. It would have required a lot of money and saving up to reach this goal. There was also a risk of you buying a bad house or a car and incurring some kind of loss. But you knew that it was something you had to do, so no matter how boring or difficult the process might have seemed, somehow you managed it. The same attitude is expected from you when you decide to do investing. This book is meant to help you, as a beginner, get started with your investment journey. To show you how to make a comfortable budget, that includes investment expenses, and gives you advice on money management.

Investment is not some far off unreachable task that only professionals can do. Not everyone that owns a car can fix it. You have to get some help at times and maybe require a lot of advice along your journey, but that is normal. Thousands of people have received enormous wealth because of investing, and they did not necessarily have a financial or business background. You just need to know the basics, hows, do's, and don'ts of trading in the financial market.

You might be confused by the numerous options presented to you for investing, but some may have too little growth, while some may be riskier than what they are worth. The best and safest option for investing, with minimal risk, is mutual funds.

Mutual funds are getting popular day by day, and for a good reason. They are highly diversified, but not too much. They can be easily traded, and based on your financial goals, can be invested by using different strategies. There are so many different types of them that there is always a fund that suits every person's needs. You can get into it by using a minuscule amount that you can afford to lose. These small amounts can grow into substantial wealth that can fuel your retirement, traveling goals, life goals, and other needs. They can help you fund your parents, spouse, or children's future and leave a better impact on their lives as well.

In this book, you have learned about mutual funds and how they work. First, the different types according to the period of investing, ultra-short, short, and long-term funds. Secondly, the types according to what kind of securities they deal with, equity, stocks, EFTs, etc. Last but not least, the types are based on whether the fund has a load or no load. Thus, you are given great and diverse choices to pick funds that will help you reach your financial goals easily. The book also gives you abundant advice on what kind of investment you should choose.

Now, you can let all this knowledge make you become a better and more prepared individual, or you can sit back on this information and let multiple opportunities pass by. There is always something happening in the mutual fund market, and every single day, there comes a new opportunity. If you take it, then your entire life can be changed. The best time to invest in mutual funds is right now. Wealth grows in mutual funds through time, and through time the risks are minimized, and you increase your chances of getting a high return. Do not sleep on this once in a lifetime chance, or else you will always regret it in the future.

Investing might leave you with a multitude of emotions. It could be excitement, which will develop by learning a new process. It could be anxiousness, which can drive from your want to do well and your perfectionist side acting up. You can get fearful and make mistakes or get greedy and acquire losses. But the most important thing is that you will never feel regret. Regret of not taking an opportunity when it was staring you right at your face, regret at not living life to the fullest and regret not giving a better life to your family.

No matter what point in life you are standing at, you can always learn a new skill or trade, such as investing. To keep improving yourself is a part of a healthy and active life. Your mindset will widen, and you will become wiser as each day passes by.

It is going to be difficult to lose money when you are investing in long-term funds, but if you do lose some money, do not be disheartened and try again with more details and experience that you have gathered now. When you invest, there is a certain risk involved with investing, so keeping that in mind, take necessary steps and avoid using your precious savings for riskier options. Always opt for the safest route available.

Once you have dived into the world of investing, do not stop learning and keep trying new things. Do not give up after slight setbacks. After you have gained experience and become a type of savant yourself, try to enrich other people's minds and teach them how to make their lives better through mutual funds.

Many of us get trapped in the wheel of life and join a 9-to-5 salary job, working hard for a company that will not think twice about firing us on the spot. You need to start planning to get out of this insane rat race as soon as possible before it devours your entire life. Use the money you acquired through investing to follow your dreams and do what you always wanted to do.

If you find this book insightful and helpful, then be sure to leave a positive review. Share it with your friends or family that are thinking about investing themselves. If you get yourself in any problem and are not sure if this book has a solution for it, then you should join a Facebook group (Investing on a Budget) that has been created to keep your investing journey moving. The group will be a great place to meet people and learn from people that are in different stages of their journey. Finally, I wish you all the best for your future. Hope that your life is filled with good investment choices and you become successful.

Index

Index fund, 28

Investment company, 66

Investment-Cum-Financial Service Companies, 66

Investment broker, 60

Interest tax, 53

IRA, 44

L

Large growth funds, 22

Liability, 9

Liquidity, 36

Load funds, 38

Long term investing, 76

M

Maintenance fees, 49

Market cap, 25

Minimum amount, 42

MER, 47

Merrill edge, 65

Money market funds, 29

Mutual funds, 25

N

NAV, 47

Net worth, 9

No load funds, 40

Non-publicly offered mutual funds, 67

O

Online investing, 68

Outstanding shares, 25

Ultra short-term mutual fund, 20

References

Ally. (2019, August 20). *Mutual Fund Fees and Expenses*. Do It Right. https://www.ally.com/do-it-right/investing/fees-and-expenses-for-mutual-funds/?chid=0.7360489413815066

Beginners Guide to Choosing Mutual Funds. (n.d.). The Balance. Retrieved July 27, 2021, from https://www.thebalance.com/best-mutual-funds-for-beginners-2466565

Benefits of ETFs - Fidelity. (n.d.-a). The Fidelity. Retrieved July 27, 2021, from http://www.fidelity.com/learning-center/investment-products/etf/benefits-of-etfs

Benefits of ETFs - Fidelity. (n.d.-b). The Fidelity. Retrieved July 27, 2021, from http://www.fidelity.com/learning-center/investment-products/etf/benefits-of-etfs

Best Online Stock Brokers for Beginners. (n.d.). Investopedia. Retrieved July 27, 2021, from https://www.investopedia.com/best-brokers-for-beginners-4587873

Best Ultra Short Funds - Top Performing Ultra Short Mutual Funds to Invest in 2021. (n.d.). Groww. Retrieved July 27, 2021, from https://groww.in/mutual-funds/category/best-ultra-short-mutual-funds

Bogart, J. (2021, May 20). *Considering No-load Mutual Funds? Read This 2021 Guide.* Bogart Wealth. http://bogartwealth.com/no-load-mutual-funds/

C. (2021, July 23). *Are Mutual Funds Safe? What Is the Risk of Investing In a Mutual Fund?* Defmacro Software Pvt. Ltd. Copyright (c) 2016. https://cleartax.in/s/mutual-funds-safe

Calculate Total Cost of ETF. (n.d.). Yahoo Finance. Retrieved July 27, 2021, from https://finance.yahoo.com/news/calculate-total-cost-etf-200030478.html?guccounter=1&guce_referrer=aH R0cHM6Ly93d3cuZ29vZ2xlLmNvbS8&guce_refer rer_sig=AQAAALk49y9QkRB3G1kFeOoM7Wf25 Kd4FB4PVP71iC_D7tZF1lLK3SRBTdBWjagEkh FusqkM0JCBwWk3f3fY48kFgiXiS1he__QikK9y2l v4DzvbwLULHgs6v6qb31GvsHfr26H8jbjbDZ322s iPnuX6uYGPmbBvk3kR3FQoolVIVXcD

Capital, P. (n.d.). *Net Worth Calculator: Know Your Net Worth.* Personal Capital. Retrieved July 27, 2021, from https://www.personalcapital.com/financial-software/net-worth?utm_medium=cpc&utm_source=google&utm_campaign=Google_Search_NB_Net%20Worth&utm_content=calculate%20my%20net%20worth&utm_device=c&gclid=CjwKCAjwtJ2FBhAuEiwAIKu19s2J3fXawggmRticbDsMESbwC9KrkOc9QB96kNk1eGeGUxndlzlVbxoC55oQAvD_BwE

Caplinger, D. (2021, July 22). *Why Do I Need a Stock Broker?* The Motley Fool. https://www.fool.com/the-ascent/buying-stocks/articles/why-do-i-need-a-stock-broker/

Carlson, D. (2021, February 26). *What to Know About the Average Rate of Return on Mutual Funds.* The Money. https://money.usnews.com/investing/investing-101/articles/what-to-know-about-the-average-rate-of-return-on-mutual-funds

CI Global Asset Management © 1997 - 2021. (n.d.). *How often should you check your portfolio? | CI Global Asset Management.* © 2021 CI Global Asset Management, All Rights Reserved. Retrieved July 27, 2021, from https://www.ci.com/en/resources/financial-literacy/how-often-should-you-check-portfolio

Contributors, E. T. (2017, September 12). *How long should long-term be in investing?* The Economic Times.

https://economictimes.indiatimes.com/wealth/invest/how-long-should-long-term-be-in-investing/articleshow/60436256.cms?from=mdr

Create a Budget and Save More Money. (n.d.). The Balance. Retrieved July 27, 2021, from https://www.thebalance.com/how-to-budget-and-save-money-in-5-easy-steps-4056838

Duff, V. (2019, February 12). *How to Cash Out a Mutual Fund Early*. Budgeting Money - The Nest. https://budgeting.thenest.com/cash-out-mutual-fund-early-27577.html

Fidelity Investments. (n.d.). The Fidelity. Retrieved July 27, 2021, from http://www.fidelity.com/tax-information/tax-topics/mutual-funds

How Are ETF Fees Deducted? (n.d.). Investopedia. Retrieved July 27, 2021, from https://www.investopedia.com/ask/answers/071816/how-are-etf-fees-deducted.asp

How to Buy Mutual Funds Online. (n.d.). Investopedia. Retrieved July 27, 2021, from https://www.investopedia.com/articles/investing/111915/looking-buy-mutual-funds-online-here-how.asp

How to Buy Mutual Funds without a Broker. (2016, March 26). Dummies.

https://www.dummies.com/personal-finance/investing/online-investing/how-to-buy-mutual-funds-without-a-broker/

Investing on Your Own | Investor.gov. (n.d.). The Investor. Retrieved July 27, 2021, from https://www.investor.gov/introduction-investing/getting-started/investing-your-own

James Royal. (2021a, February 1). *5 Ways To Use Your Brokerage Like A Savings Account*. Bankrate. https://www.bankrate.com/banking/savings/ways-to-use-broker-for-savings/

James Royal. (2021b, July 1). *7 Best Short-Term Investments In July 2021*. Bankrate. https://www.bankrate.com/investing/best-short-term-investments/

John, C. (2019, March 6). *What Is the Penalty for Early Withdrawal on Mutual Funds?* Finance - Zacks. https://finance.zacks.com/penalty-early-withdrawal-mutual-funds-8964.html

K. (2020, December 9). *What is an ETF? Advantages & Disadvantages*. Arbor Asset Allocation Model Portfolio (AAAMP) Value Blog. https://www.arborinvestmentplanner.com/what-is-an-etf-advantages-disadvantages-newsletter/

Karvy Online. (2019, August 1). *Mutual Fund Taxation - Know How are Mutual Funds Taxed in India | Karvy Online*. Karvy Stock Broking Ltd. All Rights Reserved. https://www.karvyonline.com/knowledge-center/beginner/mutual-funds/mutual-funds-taxation

Katzeff, P. (2021, June 17). *Build Your Portfolio With These Best Mutual Funds That Repeatedly Top The Market*. Investor's Business Daily. https://www.investors.com/etfs-and-funds/mutual-funds/best-mutual-funds-2021-top-funds-all-types-fill-your-portfolio/

Klimashousky, D. (2018, September 12). *What Is an Investment Broker?* SmartAsset. https://smartasset.com/financial-advisor/what-is-an-investment-broker

Large Growth. (n.d.). The Money. Retrieved July 27, 2021, from https://money.usnews.com/funds/mutual-funds/rankings/large-growth

Marquit, M. (2019, November 18). *The Smarter Mutual Fund*. The Money. https://money.usnews.com/money/blogs/the-smarter-mutual-fund-investor/articles/4-tips-to-include-investing-in-your-budget

Merrill Edge. (n.d.). *How & When Are Mutual Funds Taxed? (Capital Gains & Dividends)*. Retrieved July 27, 2021, from https://www.merrilledge.com/ask/taxes/how-are-mutual-funds-taxed

Mishra, A. (2020, August 19). *How Often Should You Check and Review Your Portfolio?* Wishfin. https://www.wishfin.com/mutual-fund/how-often-should-you-check-and-review-your-portfolio/#:%7E:text=Once%20you%20have%20made%20the,could%20lead%20to%20irrational%20decisions

Mutual Fund Definition. (n.d.). Investopedia. Retrieved July 27, 2021, from https://www.investopedia.com/terms/m/mutualfund.asp

Mutual Funds | Investor.gov. (n.d.). The Investor. Retrieved July 27, 2021, from https://www.investor.gov/introduction-investing/investing-basics/investment-products/mutual-funds-and-exchange-traded-1

Mutual Funds: Advantages and Disadvantages. (n.d.). Investopedia. Retrieved July 27, 2021, from https://www.investopedia.com/ask/answers/10/mutual-funds-advantages-disadvantages.asp

No-Load Fund Definition. (n.d.-a). Investopedia. Retrieved July 27, 2021, from https://www.investopedia.com/terms/n/no-loadfund.asp#:%7E:text=A%20no%2Dload%20fund%20is,going%20through%20a%20secondary%20party

No-Load Fund Definition. (n.d.-b). Investopedia. Retrieved July 27, 2021, from https://www.investopedia.com/terms/n/no-loadfund.asp#:%7E:text=A%20no%2Dload%20fund%20is,going%20through%20a%20secondary%20party

Non-Publicly Offered Mutual Fund. (n.d.). Investopedia. Retrieved July 27, 2021, from https://www.investopedia.com/terms/n/non-publicly-offered-mutual-funds.asp

Orem, T. (2021, February 12). *How Tax on Mutual Funds Works & 6 Ways to Cut the Bill*. NerdWallet. https://www.nerdwallet.com/article/taxes/taxes-on-mutual-funds

Perez, K. (2021, June 8). *How to Make a Budget that Works*. Investor Junkie. https://investorjunkie.com/personal-finance/build-budget/

Perez, L. C. (2018, September 5). *What Is the Minimum You Need to Invest for a Mutual Fund?* SmartAsset. https://smartasset.com/investing/mutual-fund-minimum-investment

Reinvestment. (n.d.). Investopedia. Retrieved July 27, 2021, from https://www.investopedia.com/terms/r/reinvestment.asp#:%7E:text=Reinvestment%20is%20a%20great%20way,units%20of%20the%20same%20investment

Robert, L. (2020, July 1). *15 Investing Rules To Win The Long Game*. Seeking Alpha. https://seekingalpha.com/article/4356494-15-investing-rules-to-win-long-game

Selling Mutual Funds: What Happens When You Liquidate? (n.d.). Investopedia. Retrieved July 27, 2021, from https://www.investopedia.com/articles/etfs-mutual-funds/050316/selling-mutual-funds-what-happens-when-you-liquidate.asp

Sethi, R. (2021, July 9). *How Mutual Funds Work: What are they and should you invest in them*. I Will Teach You To Be Rich. https://www.iwillteachyoutoberich.com/blog/all-about-mutual-funds/

Short Duration Funds. (n.d.). Etmoney. Retrieved July 27, 2021, from https://www.etmoney.com/mf/short-duration-mutual-funds

Should You Manage Your Own Investments or Hire a Professional? (n.d.). The Balance. Retrieved July 27, 2021, from https://www.thebalance.com/should-you-manage-your-own-investments-358167

Staff, M. F. (2016, November 28). *Can Anyone Create a Mutual Fund?* The Motley Fool. https://www.fool.com/knowledge-center/can-anyone-create-a-mutual-fund.aspx

Staff, T. C. D. (2021, July 23). *Home*. The Columbus Dispatch. https://eu.dispatch.com/

Tretina, K. (2020, December 21). *How To Invest In Mutual Funds*. Forbes Advisor. https://www.forbes.com/advisor/investing/how-to-invest-in-mutual-funds/

Voigt, K. (2021, May 24). *Mutual Fund Fees: A Guide for Beginners*. NerdWallet. https://www.nerdwallet.com/article/investing/mutual-fund-fees-what-investors-need-to-know

What Is Net Worth? (n.d.). The Balance. Retrieved July 27, 2021, from https://www.thebalance.com/what-is-your-net-worth-1289788

What Is the Average Mutual Fund Return? (n.d.). The Balance. Retrieved July 27, 2021, from https://www.thebalance.com/what-is-the-average-mutual-fund-return-4773782

What to Consider When Starting a Mutual Fund. (n.d.-a). Investopedia. Retrieved July 27, 2021, from https://www.investopedia.com/articles/mutualfund/11/build-own-mutual-fund.asp

What to Consider When Starting a Mutual Fund. (n.d.-b). Investopedia. Retrieved July 27, 2021, from https://www.investopedia.com/articles/mutualfund/11/build-own-mutual-fund.asp

Why Are ETF Fees Lower Than Mutual Fund Fees? (n.d.). Investopedia. Retrieved July 27, 2021, from https://www.investopedia.com/articles/investing/102915/why-are-etf-fees-lower-mutual-funds.asp

Your 6-Step Guide to Making a Personal Budget. (n.d.). The Balance. Retrieved July 27, 2021, from https://www.thebalance.com/how-to-make-a-budget-1289587

Your Personal Net Worth. (n.d.). Schwabmoneywise. Retrieved July 27, 2021, from https://www.schwabmoneywise.com/public/money wise/essentials/personal_net_worth

Made in the USA
Middletown, DE
16 January 2022

58814249R00102